Possibly because the name embraces the term 'public', people generally associate the republic with democracy. It is as well to know that in its origins in ancient Rome, and in its most prominent present-day example in the United States, it has nothing practical to do with democracy. The central idea of the republic is ruling without a king, and when the Romans expelled their kings, their place was taken by wealthy landholders in turn, while the common people were held as far from political power as possible. Republican Rome, from start to chaotic finish, was ruled by an oligarchy of wealth. When the United States was founded, its founding 'fathers' hated democracy almost to a man, and they established institutions to keep the ordinary person as far away from political power as possible. America is unequivocally ruled by elites of the wealthy, and the system is geared to keeping it that way.

In Australia our republican advocates like Malcolm Turnbull, Tom Keneally and Peter FitzSimons seem to care little for the history of republicanism, but we should all be aware that concepts drawn from history are freighted with experience which may be absorbed into our own structures. The current shining example of republic means nothing less than 'rule by the rich'.

The
Rich
Tradition
of
Republicanism

Graham Maddox is Professor Emeritus of political science at the University of New England. He is a Fellow of the Academy of Social Sciences in Australia, a member of Clare Hall, Cambridge and of the Center of Theological Inquiry at Princeton NJ. He is author of *Australian Democracy in Theory and Practice*, 5th ed. 2005; *The Hawke Government and Labor Tradition*, 1989; *Religion and the Rise of Democracy*, 2015; *Stepping Up to the Plate. America, and Australian Democracy*, 2016, and numerous other writings on Australian politics and the history of political thought.

The
Rich
Tradition
of
Republicanism

GRAHAM MADDOX

PAMPHLETEER

Pamphleteer is an Australian Scholarly imprint.

First published 2016 by Australian Scholarly Publishing Pty Ltd
7 Lt Lothian St Nth, North Melbourne, Vic 3051
TEL: 03 9329 6963   FAX: 03 9329 5452
EMAIL: aspic@ozemail.com.au   WEB: scholarly.info

ISBN 978-1-925333-85-5

Contents

Introduction

Republicanism has a rich history – rich being the operative word. If we take the alpha and omega of the republican tradition, its origin in ancient Rome, and its hegemonic present exemplar, the United States, it is evident that both were set up by rich magnates in direct opposition to the 'common herd' of the general population. The Roman republic ended in disaster and tyranny, while the wealth elites of the United States continue to exploit its republican constitution in ever narrowing circles of the powerful and the ever-widening obscenity of their wealth. The tide of literature that emerged during the campaign for an Australian republic in the 1990s was largely innocent of an international debate on the nature of republican history.

The current chair of the Australian Republican Movement, Peter FitzSimons, continues the mantra set up by Malcolm Turnbull two decades ago: 'we want an Australian as head of state'. This sounds more like the flutter of national insecurity, akin to the flag waving and chest thumping of white Australians on Invasion Day, than a sensible contribution to political understanding. There is a nationalist murmur in the stirrings of Australian republicanism, while full-throated nationalism is a most unattractive ideology.[1] Hereditary monarchy is indeed indefensible, but few Australian commentators tell us why in principle this is so. One does not have to be a monarchist to see that the modern conversation on an Australian republic has dangerously shallow foundations.

Internationally published works by Bill Brugger, Patricia Springborg and Philip Pettit were exceptions to republican parochialism in that they addressed wider traditions, but they had hardly any impact on the local debate. Another exception, distinguished by his careful analysis of republican impulses in Australian history, was Mark McKenna. George Winterton, greatly incensed by the injustice and unconstitutionality of the Whitlam dismissal in 1975, proposed elaborate republican reforms as befitted a distinguished constitutional lawyer. Australia's most recognizable international author, Tom Keneally, a passionate republican from birth, it would seem, was prevailed upon to become the first chair of a new Australian republican movement, and wrote a chatty, engaging account of the event in a book with the unlikely dust-cover caption 'The most important book about Australia since *The Fatal Shore*'.[2]

An Australian Republic?

The more passionate of the Australian republicans seem to think that any criticism of the republican idea must imply a sentimental attachment to the monarchy. This is not the case here. First, this is NOT a monarchist tract. All the republican claims about the silliness of allegiance to the British crown and loyalty to the empire and the British commonwealth are obvious and valid. Some critics are content that the recent governors-general, in effect heads of the Australian state, have been Australians. (At least one of them could have been chosen more carefully.)

Yet there remains some confusion about what is meant by a republic. The leading constitutional theorist of the republican movement, George Winterton, gave us workable accounts. One ran like this: 'A republic is a state based upon popular sovereignty, in which all public power is exercised by the people or by the persons and institutions chosen by them, directly or indirectly.'[3] Alastair Davidson thought that the *res publica* ('the people's business') idea was scarcely helpful in an age where 'popular sovereignty' had little content, but suggested that a republic 'denotes a polity where the active political decision-making is directed to securing the citizens' collective interest or good, which are not necessarily the same thing.'[4] Unlike many other commentators, Davidson is fully aware of the historical context of the idea, but his notion of *res publica* is vitiated by his acceptance of a widespread misconception that republicanism originated in the Greek city-states.[5]

Both Winterton and Davidson lack one thing in their approaches. If republicanism means anything, it means dispensing with monarchy, as was the case with historical republics. The Australian republicans are quite right to be impatient with those who, like J.B. Paul, Michael Kirby and David Flint, pronouncing Australia a 'crowned republic', were following Walter Bagehot's outlandish sophism that 'a Republic has insinuated itself beneath the folds of a Monarchy'.[6] It is the removal of the monarchy that is central to what it means to have a republic. The history does matter. A few of our commentators recognize the fact. Political words are shorthand for experience. The term 'democracy' only exists because Greek states once determined to experiment with citizens ruling themselves. The idea of a state emerges when Renaissance Italy evolves a communal welfare from an 'estate' of a monarch. 'Sovereignty' can only properly be understood when we know why Hobbes in England and Bodin in France experienced the need to define such an idea. Helen Irving recognizes the historical freight borne by the Australian founders' selection of 'Commonwealth' as the style for the new federation. At least, she says, Alfred Deakin had an eye to the interregnum ruled by Cromwell in the eighteenth century after the removal of the monarch's head.[7]

If republicanism is not recognized in its historical context, then it is nothing. The word itself is simply a generic word for 'the state'. It was used to translate Plato's *Politeia* into Latin, thus rendering for all time the title of Plato's famous work as 'The Republic'; but Plato's conception was nothing at all like the form of government evolved in Rome after the expulsion of the kings, the event that gave us our first outline of republicanism. We shall soon see that, despite the high-flown rhetoric, the republic of Rome had nothing practical at all to do with Winterton's idea of popular sovereignty 'in which all public power is exercised by the people or by the persons and institutions chosen by them, directly or indirectly'.

Yet Malcolm Turnbull, chairman of the Australian Republican Movement from 1993 to 2000, would have none of it. For him the republic had nothing to do with either history or political theory. (I once heard him say to my then colleague, Alan Atkinson, that 'history is bunk'.) His term as chairperson covered the period of the ill-fated 1999 referendum on the republic, and I dare say his lack of leadership contributed largely to its failure (combined, of course, with the machinations of the then prime minister, John Howard, who contrived to turn populism on its head and court traditional Labor supporters). The broadsheet press labelled those who voted against the republic as 'uneducated'.[8] When I say 'lack of leadership', I cannot deny that Turnbull was hugely visible, trumpeting his endless cry that we need an Australian as head of state. We all heard that *ad nauseam.* Turnbull explicitly rejected any explanation of the term 'republic': '… not a lot is to be gained by semantic discussions about what is a republic …' He then restated, 'The republican debate is about having an Australian head of state, that is all.'[9] He explicitly advised his republican colleagues *not to debate the issues*, fearing 'primitive alarmism' from opponents such as Bronwyn Bishop.[10]

In his own book Turnbull declared that 'The republic is about nothing more than asserting our national identity.'[11] This could well serve as an epigrammatic review of the book itself. Turnbull manages to churn out 358 pages on a 'reluctant republic' without including any republican content at all. With perhaps one exception. And that turns out to be a massive contradiction to his own stand. The republican cause, he says, is 'truly radical'. 'It is radical because it is genuinely democratic and because it is unprecedented in our society.'[12] If he meant by this that 'democracy' was unprecedented, he may have astonished his distinguished colleague, George Winterton. Yet he said nothing to justify or explain this bold claim, and was not going to let the people in on his idea of democracy; so he rolled on into his condescending polemic against 'smug' opponents. Little wonder that the republic was 'reluctant'.

Discussing what terms really mean to us cannot be wiped off as merely 'semantic'. There is a powerful body of literature that demonstrates how our language shapes our attitudes and can change policies and alter institutions. Take for example James Boyd White's magnificent *When Words Lose Their Meaning. Constitutions and Reconstitutions of Language, Character, and Community*.[13] Turnbull made the fatal mistake of not realizing that people really wanted to know what a change to a republic would entail. The new language of politics could well reconstitute Australia as a new type of community, perhaps in further emulation of the republic of the United States. That change would be fraught with danger, as I intend to argue.

Turnbull's lack of leadership was evident on two fronts. First, he failed to recognize that if the people were to vote at referendum on changing to a republic, they would want to know what shape that new polity would actually take. Turnbull hoped his minimalist stand, simply to cut ties with the British crown and change the governor-generalship into a presidency, would be acceptable. Yet, if you are to mobilize the people to vote for a change in the constitution, would you not anticipate that, having excited their passion so (to use Madison's quaint turn of phrase), they would want to be involved in choosing who the new president should be? Would not then an elected president introduce the possibility of a radical change to the governmental system?

Worse than all of that, however, Turnbull showed contempt for the Australian people. Too many of them knew that a republic meant much more than having an Australian as head of state. Even the words Turnbull used were loaded with implication: of course, moving to an Australian head of state would mean removing the monarchy, and that would have to mean a serious change in the constitution. I am not here saying that such a move was not worth a try. The point is that such a change would and should involve the people in partnership, and nothing Turnbull did during the campaign showed any respect for the people's judgment. They were not to learn the implications of a republic, and were treated like fools. By contrast, John Warhurst lamented 'the appalling ignorance which surrounds public discussion of the issue ...'[14]

It cannot be ignored that some of the reactions of the monarchists were indeed silly. There were stories about republicans being shunned by former friends, being expelled from clubs, fearing dismissal from their posts or losing their clients. Among the more outlandish was the reaction of that well-known redneck bespangled with imperial and Australian honours, Bruce Ruxton, at the time president of the Victorian Returned Services League. He called for the arrest of Tom Keneally, Neville Wran and Malcolm Turnbull under some obscure sedition legislation. Ruxton's line was that Australians had given their lives in military service to the crown, empire and the Australian flag. Tom was not going to let Ruxton off the hook, and countered with reports of Australian soldiers showing their contempt for British officers and expressing no enthusiasm for fighting for the empire.[15] Loyalty to the British crown was at the heart of monarchist sentiment, and it was usually accompanied with comforting thoughts about being safe in the alliance and being able to call on imperial forces for our defence. Donald Horne effectively demolished the utility of 'loyalty' for any practical purposes. Countries to whom we were loyal were always going to put their own interests before ours, and it was the responsibility of an independent nation to negotiate in its own interests as the situation required.[16]

On the other hand, some of the responses to monarchist taunting were really over the top. Keneally called the monarchy 'an amalgam of magic and atavism'. He is complicit also in one of the famous misquotations about Robert Menzies, who was undoubtedly lavish in his expressions of love for the young Queen during her visits to Australia. Repeatedly we have been told that he was speaking for himself when he said 'I did but see her passing by, and yet I love her till I die'. He was quoting a line of the seventeenth century poet Thomas Ford's 'There is a lady sweet and fair', made famous in a song setting by Edward Purcell.[17] These may well have been Menzies's own sentiments, but that is not what he said. Menzies claimed to be speaking for the unfortunate crowds who did not get to meet the Queen in person. On her second royal visit in 1963 he said to her: 'All I ask you to remember in this country of yours is that every man, woman and child who even sees you with a passing glimpse as you go by will remember it, remember it with joy, remember it – in the words of the old 17th century poet who wrote those famous words, "I did but see her passing by and yet I love her till I die."'[18]

Tom Keneally is anxious to rule out either race or sectarianism as a republican issue. His Irish heritage was not a cause of his republicanism. Yet he makes a great deal of his Irishness and the contempt his immediate forebears had for Britain and the monarchy. The Irish Christian Brothers who taught him at school had no time for the English establishment, while his 'tribe' was in combat with the Masons. He is quick to say that most of his co-founders of the modern republican movement were not Irish, and that he and Geraldine Doogue were exceptions. Another prominent republican, Sister Veronica Brady, was glad to dispense with British ties. In an interview with Myfanwy Gollan she was asked: 'You ask why canonise the people who shipped out so many of your ancestors?'[19] These sentiments were surely not alien to Tom Keneally. When Catholics were accused of disloyalty to the crown because of their allegiance to a pope resident in Italy, Keneally was careful to point out that the pope is not an element of the Australian constitution, while 'the Monarchy still – shamefully for us – claims our total loyalty'.[20]

'Canonise' was an interesting word. Keneally is surely over the top when he offers the Queen as a substitute female deity for protestant conservatives. 'Religion does tend to female deities, willy nilly.' Interestingly, he implies that the Madonna was a deity, perhaps echoing those speculations that made Mary, the mother of Jesus, a continuing substitute for the once universal goddess, Isis. In the Queen, however, 'here was a female deity suitable for the withering ennui of Australia in the 1950s'.[21] Talk about Menzies!

There is a deep contradiction in the republican attitude to pre-republican Australia. Keneally's Australian 'ennui' of the 1950s strikes an echo of Donald Horne's tiredness with Menzian Australia expressed in *The Lucky Country*. The place is boring, unimaginative, lacklustre and drab. The republicans stress Australia's failure to grow up. Geraldine Doogue was contemptuous, pinning the general lack of a distinctive identity on the monarchists, who practise 'avoidance on a massive scale'. 'Please let me stay home with Mum because I don't want to face the world'. Behind this, she said, was a fearful Australian community, 'traumatized by change and trembling in anticipation of more.'[22]

Keneally is perturbed by the adolescence of Australia, and presses the growing up theme relentlessly. He quotes with approval Les Murray's affirmation of the theme, where the absentee monarch, 'what I call the mercantile protectorate', holds down our energies and creativity. The connection with the English royal family is a 'disease'. 'The Crown remains what it always has been, a psychic weapon held in benign reserve *against our growing up and finding ourselves.*'[23] Tom Keneally was content to talk about 'our lust for dependence on others'.

He embodied the contradiction in his ARM launch speech:

> We came to feel we possessed both an inherent wor-
> thiness which would assure that others – our betters –
> would look after us; and an inherent inferiority which
> convinced us we were not worthy to manage ourselves
> or speak with an utterly independent voice. Both these
> suspicions are delusions and have damaged us and have
> kept us a stunted nation … If we cannot find loyalty,
> sanity and human decency amongst ourselves, then we
> are finished.[24]

The contradiction is plain: Australia is ready to stand on her own two feet and seek true independence (which we do not have);[25] at the same time we are grovelling in cultural cringe, deluded, unsure of our identity and clinging to dependence on outside champions. Australians are 'second class citizens'.[26] Changing our style to a republic, without changing any of our constitutional arrangements as Turnbull would have it, would cure everything overnight. It is the monarchy that is to blame for all our uncertainty and hesitancy.

According to Donald Horne, giving an adverse assessment of royal visitors usurping honorary tasks that should have been offered to Australians, the monarchy is an enemy of democra-cy.[27] Malcolm Turnbull asserted that Australian democracy owed 'nothing to the Queen. The Queen is a symbol, a symbol without substance'.[28] This is absurd. I repeat what I acknowledged at the beginning, that there is no justification for lifelong rule to be vested in a single person, nor for heredity as qualification for rul-ership. But this affirmation is no warrant for historical blindness, or for the emptiness of the black letter lawyer. The generality of rule throughout history has been the imposition of government by force and the concentration of power in the hands of some violent individual. Both republicanism and democracy evolved from the struggle to get rid of the rule of tyrants. Democracy in the model of ancient Athens meant replacing the power of the tyrant with rule by the people themselves. The situation was quite otherwise with the model republic in Rome.

The Australian republican anti-monarchic case relies heavily upon the multicultural argument that not all Australians are of British descent, and that many, such as Franca Arena, find it curious and repellent to swear allegiance to the British Queen. Fair enough. But no such argument can obliterate the fact that the institutions of Australian government, which are the target of republican change, derived from British institutions that had evolved over centuries of gradual democratic development. The monarchy is the counterpoint to the democratic theme, the integral irritant of an evolving democracy. There is no point in rehearsing the British case for the utility of the monarchy – its unity, its focus of national loyalty, its position above the ordinary interplay of politics, its accumulated experience – since I have already expressed an aversion to hereditary and permanent rule.

Nevertheless there is something majestic (used advisedly) in the importation of the British evolved rule of law, as rough and ready as it may have appeared at first in the colonies, in the formation of an Australian nation. When the republicans assert a certain robust fairness in the Australian character, at least some of it is attributable to this inheritance of the rule of law.[29] As for the monarchy, whatever else is said about it, it is the British throne (along with Scandinavian ones) that, over centuries, has withdrawn, or been withdrawn, from the arena of force, has as-

12

sumed that, aloof from everyday politics 'the Queen can do no wrong', that has been a model for constitutional government. Most significantly, Patricia Springborg reminds us that the modern welfare state grew up 'under the wings of old monarchies rather than new republics'.[30] It is cheeky indeed to say that this is an empty symbol, that it is anti-democratic. It may be one that we consciously reject, but it has its historical significance, and as Springborg suggests, it is as well to remember that any constitutional change should ensure that not all is lost from the benevolences of the past.

The Dismissal

The dismissal of the elected government of Australia by the un-elected Queen's representative in 1975 undoubtedly set people a-thinking about the validity of our present constitution, and many turned towards a republican solution. Whether it was acknowledged by the key players or not, the governor-general's precipitate action had to have been done in the Queen's name. It seemed to follow that the immediate remedy would be to cut all ties to the crown.

Tom Keneally, while acknowledging the impetus for change from the dismissal, was careful to point out that the republic was the future of Australia regardless of particular political events. (For shame, Gough Whitlam, a committed republican, was passed over by the movement because of his Labor affiliation.) Indeed, there had been calls to enact Australian independence under a republican constitution from the start of the colony. This was undoubtedly with an eye to American independence and its brand new constitution promulgated the year before the first fleet landed in Port Jackson. After all, Britain had been transporting convicts to American colonies before that avenue was cut off by the American War of Independence. New South Wales became the substitute prison. British authorities both 'at home' and in the colony were fearful of the spread of civil violence engendered by the French Revolution, breaking out one year after the landing of the first fleet. New South Wales was born in turbulent times.

Mark McKenna tells the wonderful story of the convict, Joseph Smallsorts, who was *transported* from Sydney Cove to Newcastle NSW for his seditious crimes in 1806. He had boasted of his sympathy with Thomas Paine, the Norfolk republican who had successive influence on the revolutions in both America and France. Smallsorts was flogged for his subversive opinions, and sent down the mines.[31] McKenna gives a comprehensive account of early intimations of colonial republicanism, but the first full flowering of the idea came in the 1850s, especially with the agitations of John Dunmore Lang.

The first Presbyterian minister in the colony, Lang was 'the person most responsible for forcing the issue of an Australian republic into the mainstream of political discussion in the 1850s'. McKenna explains Lang's irritation with British colonial authorities in undermining his attempts to build a strong Presbyterian clergy in Australia, and demonstrates his chartist sympathies, which helped set him on a republican path.[32] Lang was also a huge America-phile, and in 1840 he travelled to America, touring along the eastern seaboard. 'Manners were simple, aristocratic pretensions were unknown, morals pure and religion and education well-supported in these small, self-governing communities.' Like the Irish, Lang the Scot from Glasgow had little love for the English establishment, while 'as a Presbyterian he strongly resented the social privileges and religious pretensions of the Church of England'.[33] Moreover, he was constantly at war with the Catholics. Patrick O'Farrell called him, 'that tempestuous, acidulated

Presbyterian minister who regarded the Pope as the Man of Sin, and local Catholics as his diabolical minions plotting to dominate New South Wales'.[34] It should be added that Lang was also contemptuous of most of his fellow Dissenters.

Lang's enduring reputation rests on his advocacy of republicanism. The term was bandied about by opponents of Governor Gipps, but McKenna observes that the attitude of the squatters, desiring an elitist republic, was so much bluster about the prowess of outback horsemen and their flaunted ability to best a regiment of British troopers. Rebellion was in the air, but only till the squatters got what they wanted anyway from the government.[35] Lang's work in New South Wales was interspersed with numerous visits to the UK where he quarrelled with the colonial authorities. His visit to the United States was 'to investigate how its churches managed without government support'.[36] Deeply impressed by the atmosphere of freedom and, reflecting on the trials of Port Phillip and Moreton Bay, he admired the degree of local autonomy among the states of the American federation. In 1850 he launched a full-blown campaign for a separated, republican Australia. His considered lectures, oft repeated, 'constitute the first comprehensive argument for an Australian republic'.[37] The lectures were then published in pamphlet form.[38]

Lang's campaigns met much hostility, not least from migrants who claimed to have been swindled in the migration deal with him. He was imprisoned in Melbourne on just such a complaint. Meeting his opposition full on, he later stood for election to fill a vacancy in the Legislative Council, and was elected to great public acclaim, the first 'uncloseted republican' to hold elective office.[39] The *Sydney Morning Herald* mounted a concerted attack on him. In 1852 he completed his *magnum opus* on republicanism, *Freedom and Independence for the Golden Lands of Australia.*[40] Lang's ambition was to match *Common Sense,* Tom Paine's republican tract that ignited the American population for revolution. Yet Lang was no deist like Paine, but argued that the remote British rule over the colonies was 'against the ordinance of God'. The visit to America, Lang's admiration for most things American and his emulation of Paine led much modern commentary to the conclusion that he was entirely motivated by his fascination with America, especially when some ignore the fact that he had anything to do with the church.[41]

Such a picture glosses over the fact that Lang stood by the Westminster Confession, the product of the fierce English civil war between puritan dissenters and the Anglican establishment under Charles I.[42] The great eighteenth-century religious revival in America had radical political implications. As Gordon Wood explains:

> Although the Great Awakening commonly represented an effort by people to bring some order to their disrupted lives, its implications were radical, especially since supernatural religion remained for most ordinary people, if not for enlightened gentry, the major means of explaining the world. By challenging clerical unity, shattering the communal churches, and cutting people loose from ancient bonds, the religious revivals became in one way or another a massive defiance of traditional authority.[43]

King George III himself declared the American revolution to be 'a Presbyterian war'.[44] In 1774 an American loyalist wrote to a London newspaper, 'Believe me, the Presbyterians have been the chief and principal instruments in all these flaming measures, and they always do and ever will act against Government, from that restless and turbulent anti-monarchical spirit which has always distinguished them every where.'[45] As Sheldon Wolin comments: '… the Great Awakenings helped to further believers' democratic impulses and to urge them into the forefront of the fight against slavery'.[46] Restless and turbulent Dunmore Lang was, but the influence on him was as a pincer: American republicanism, instructed by a lingering puritan ideology hostile to kings and aristocrats,[47] and Scottish Presbyterianism together.

Lang's republicanism was quite possibly the only fully informed republican movement in our history. At least he was closely connected to the wider cause of republicanism manifested in American history, and had his campaign succeeded, that American association may have been deeply damaging to Australian democracy. With federation the republican zeal tended to wane, as the founders sought independence while maintaining loyalty to the Queen. Helen Irving, one of the few recent Australian authors to consider republicanism in relation to its wider history, shows that the federation story is not exactly anti-republican, since for the British statesman and theorist, James Harrington, 'commonwealth', the style adopted for federated Australia, was a synonym for 'republic', and bore reference to the period of Cromwell's Britain without a king.

Modern republican sensibilities were aroused by Geoffrey Dutton in 1963. He and Donald Horne were then virtually lone voices, but Dutton suffered most from ostracism and rejection because of his beliefs, a brigadier even telling him to go back to Russia where he belonged. The 1975 dismissal was a goad for a campaign of renewed vigour, since the Australian 'mental half-sleep was temporarily jerked wide awake' by Kerr's folly.[48] Elaine Thompson saw in it a chance to change the constitution of Australia for the better.[49]

There is no doubt that the arbitrary dismissal of the Whitlam government exposed serious weaknesses in the way politics was done in this country.[50] The republicans were keen to root the cause of the problem to the monarchy, because Whitlam was dismissed by the Queen's man, John Kerr. It would be just as correct to say that Kerr was Whitlam's man, because he had been appointed on Whitlam's advice to the crown.

The deluge of literature on the dismissal of 1975 fully exposes a governor-general of flawed character, concerned far more about the safety of his own position, his own manufactured sense of dignity, his reputation among men of real substance in the community (not the working-class rabble that put him there) and his place in history, than he ever did about the good and stable running of the country. He was home-grown, an actual Australian as quasi head of state. Kerr added nothing to help the case that Australia would be better off with 'an Australian as head of state'.

To his credit, Turnbull recognized 'that whatever had gone wrong in 1975, it had nothing to do with the Queen'.[51] Moreover, his summary account of the dismissal is accurate and balanced (despite his book's lack of specific republican content).[52] Still, the opportunity of possibly changing the constitution had presented itself.

Speaking of the constitution, Keneally expects his readers to be enraged and astounded by his revelations about its content. He then unfolds sixteen pages of absurd exposition of the literal clauses of the constitution. With his customary whimsy, Donald Horne described Kerr's manipulation of the constitution as constructing a 'governor-generalate'.[53] To be fair, anything Keneally said could not be as stupid as John Kerr's self-serving black-letter claims about his powers under the constitution, and Keneally's account is in its effect infinitely less dangerous. Nevertheless, Tom takes it to be that the governor-general is literally ruler of the state and commander-in-chief of the armed forces. He makes the 'astounding' claim that 'at the heart of our founding document, the fantasy [is] that we are a feudal people'.[54] The irony of all this was that those of us who were incensed by the injustice and constitutional destruction of the dismissal at the time presented the same facts about the constitution precisely to argue that *it was not like that*.[55] No country with any pretensions to democracy could ever be governed by the literal clauses of the constitution.

It is at this point that the history of the monarchy becomes essentially relevant to Australia, and can be no empty symbol. Keneally returns the sneers of constitutional lawyers 'who chuckle indulgently and speak of convention when Australian layfolk get upset about the prerogatives and powers awarded the Monarch under the constitution.'[56] He then dispenses with 'convention'. Yet there is no workable constitution at all without convention: there is no prime minister, no political parties, no cabinet, in the written constitution, yet all of these institutions are central to the constitutional system of government, by convention.

The madness of Kerr's action was plain when he said that convention must submit to the black letter of the constitution, yet his dismissal declaration stated that a prime minister who cannot secure supply must resign 'according to the principles of responsible government [i.e. convention]'. His muddleheadedness would be as amusing as the wombat's had not he been acting on pernicious motives to distort the constitution.[57] He had lied to his elected prime minister, Whitlam, when he told him that he did not believe in the 'reserve powers' of the governor-general, the very powers that he claimed to exert in the dismissal. Jenny Hocking has documented this duplicity in full detail.[58] Where are these 'reserve powers' in the written constitution?

One of the most startling revelations of Hocking's researches was the extent of the conspiracy on the part of the political establishment surrounding Kerr's actions. The leader of the opposition, Fraser, the chief justice, Barwick, another justice of the high court, Mason, were all involved in the conspiracy to dismiss Whitlam, and a secondary conspiracy between Barwick and Kerr to conceal the identity of Mason as a chief personal adviser to Kerr, against all vice-regal protocol, held good for a long time.[59]

At the time of his writing *The Reluctant Republic*, neither Malcolm Turnbull nor anyone else had any idea of the complicity of the palace in Kerr's folly. Malcolm's winsome but unwitting faith in the distance of the crown from the Australian crisis unravelled with the discovery of new information. Most shocking of all the revelations was the monarch's failure to keep a constitutional distance from the political machinations in Canberra, as all believed she should have. Kerr's archives show that he had made the Queen fully aware of his intentions, and that he had discussed the possibility of dismissing the government with the heir apparent. Prince Charles even hinted that the Queen would take the personal advice of the governor-general over that of the prime minister.[60] So the crisis was all-Australian made, but the ramifications were wide, and disturbing in the extreme. The implications for constitutional government were enormous, and the constitutional mess has never been resolved.

Yet did the crisis mean that the 1901 constitution was essentially flawed? That treasure fell into the hands of pirates has no bearing on the value of the treasure. Let's not be too dramatic about this. The constitution was framed in the nineteenth century, but its orientation towards 'responsible government' was clearly trending to democracy.

Keneally's representation of the constitutional document as a remit for a tyrant was at odds with the most thoughtful, and best informed, of the modern republicans, George Winterton. As he declared: 'Since our Constitution was approved by the electors before enactment at Westminster and can be amended only through a popular referendum, Australia's constitutional system is clearly already founded politically upon popular sovereignty.'[61]

Winterton goes on to claim that the Australian system, as it is, is much more based on popular sovereignty than is the American. His case for a republic is elaborated in detail in his important book, *Monarchy to Republic*, but his preference is for cutting ties with the British/Australian monarchy while disturbing our present constitutional arrangements as little as possible.[62] Colin Howard further explains: 'The draftsmen of the constitution took responsible government, or cabinet government to give it another name, for granted. They also recognized however that it is not easy to reduce such a constantly changing and evolving political concept to a strict constitutional formula. They therefore adopted the basically sensible device of sketching in the formal position of the crown and the governor-general on the assumption that the realities of government in a parliamentary system could be taken for granted.'[63]

The Wider Republican Context

Among those, besides Winterton, Irving and McKenna, who are sensitive to the wider international context of the republican idea, are Gregory Melleuish, Wayne Hudson, Andrew Fraser, Alastair Davidson, Patricia Springborg, Bill Brugger and Philip Pettit. Melleuish recognizes that republicanism was a long-established body of theory, but he rather misfires when he considers that there was a 'transition' from the Roman republic to the empire because of the inability of republican institutions to rule wide territories.[64] This is indeed part of the story but, as we shall see, the republican 'transition' was actually an eruption of violent chaos and collapse into total failure. Hudson focuses on James Harrington, whose utopian republicanism echoed widely in historical debates, while Davidson wonders at the Australian founders, who, in their overweening Anglophilia, were innocent of continental European theory.[65]

Patricia Springborg's magisterial *Western Republicanism and the Oriental Prince* mounts a fundamental challenge to the 'orientalist' orientation of western republicanism, criticizing the characterization of peoples to the east of Europe variously as barbarians and as slavish subjects of despots. Her criticism has strong resonance for today's troubles, where Europe seeks to come to terms with Islam. A chief feature of republicanism is oligarchy, while the characterization of oriental despotism as akin to totalitarianism 'reminds us that Western economic acquisitiveness has reached correspondingly gargantuan proportions, that it needs such a spectre to legitimize it'.[66]

Not really concerned with ancient republicanism, Bill Brugger concentrates on a new republicanism beginning with Machiavelli's secularized transformation of 'virtue', and rolling through distinct phases such as enlightenment republicanism, the American experiment and contemporary republicanism chiefly characterized by Philip Pettit and Quentin Skinner. The distinctive feature of republican theory, he concludes, 'is a view of political life which affirms popular sovereignty, is sensitive to corruptibility, asserts the value of civic virtue and upholds a view of liberty as non-domination.'[67]

Philip Pettit's central tenet is a theory of republicanism that engenders freedom as 'non-domination'.[68] The idea derives from an ancient Roman distinction between 'slave' and 'not-slave', which he sources to Cicero. Yet he also is little interested in the actual politics of ancient Rome that generated the republican idea. He steers a path between communitarianism and radical liberalism with a brand of republicanism that is intended as a corrective for the extremes. His 'non-domination' is intended to be a corrective to the liberal concept of liberty as 'non-interference'. He would prefer to see the power to interfere, such as a benevolent despot would have, removed or structurally contained. The operative idea here is the contestation of power, which should be dispersed so much as to render domination impossible. This raises questions about government, which under certain circumstances must 'dominate' – in emergencies for example; but the need for welfare and transfer payments for the needy becomes policies that are coercive to some. Moreover, as we see in the United States at the present, the dispersal of power may render necessary collective action impossible, and so many authors have complained about the deadlock of democracy in America. Moreover, Pettit displays a distinct aversion to 'populism' and participatory democracy, leaving the field open to the rule of elites, even if they are dispersed. Where is the *res publica,* the people's affair, in all this?

To return to the Australians of the ARM, it is significant that in his general enthusiasm for republicanism, Tom Keneally is aware of the unfortunate turn of events in the United States. He lived in the States from time to time and was able to observe at first hand: 'The United States was a Republic that was not working. *But the reason it wasn't working was not that it was a Republic.* It was not working because of its *laissez-faire* assumptions. It was not working because the institution of slavery still haunted and damned and limited it.'[69] It is the ARM's minimalist approach to the republic that leads him to this statement, but a more historical understanding of republican evolution would demonstrate that the failings he notices were built into the republic of the United States. This we shall examine shortly, but first, it is important that we observe more closely how the term, and the idea, of the republic first arose.

Ancient Rome: The Origin of the Republic

It is true that many of the writers of republican history associate the republic with the Greek city-states, which were minutely classified by Aristotle. Yet 'republic' did not, and could not appear in his matrix. Roman republicanism emerged as a distinct set of institutions alien to Greece. The most important parallel is that, according to the historical tradition, the democracy of Athens and the republic of Rome arose at about the same time, in the last decade of the sixth century B.C. Both were getting rid of 'tyrant' monarchs. Although Patricia Springborg has much to say about the stigmatization of the Greek tyrants in particular,[70] yet the regimes that replaced them were radically different as between Rome and Athens; the latter supplied us with the term 'democracy' and was an experiment with rule by the citizens, whereas Rome had a population layered and structured so that the magnates were able to keep rule firmly in their own hands.

The uprising against the last Etruscan king from Rome, recorded as being in 509 B.C., was apparently an episode in the general decline of Etruscan power at the time. Of course the last was stigmatized as a tyranny, and the Romans determined to do without monarchy forever, so hated did *rex*, the word for king, become. Anyone who aspired to overweening power was denigrated as aiming to become an accursed *rex*. Monarchy was replaced by a new idea, the *res publica*, which Cicero characterized as the *res populi*, the affair of the people.[71]

Yet this ideological slogan served as a cover for the true exercise of power, what the Romans were later to call the *arcana imperii*, the secret ways power could be exercised. Tarquinius Superbus had been expelled by powerful landlords, the fathers of substantial families and households ruling wide territories. We may assume that they would have liked the power of a king, but were not prepared to allow any one of them to take an office, *rex,* that would become anathema. The household rulers, the *patricii*, were a tight-knit caste of the privileged and wealthy, who even prevented the watering down of their order by a law that prevented intermarriage with people of the common sort, collectively known as the *plebs*.

Why then did their formulation of the new constitutional arrangement include 'the people' at all, since it was clear that the people were not to be included in any significant way in ruling themselves? Because from the start, Rome was an armed camp, and people were required to populate the armies needed to defend the state. So it was that eventually the standards that were carried into battle did honour to the people, at least in so far as the males among them were soldiers. They bore the letters *SPQR* – The Senate and the People of Rome (*senatus populusque Romanus*). The senate was the haven of the *patricii*, their ruling institution, and till the end of the republic the senate was almost always in full command.

28

With the removal of monarchy, the state nevertheless needed executive rule, and this devolved onto the office of 'consul'. It marks the chief characteristic of the republic, because it is the antithesis of monarchy. This is embodied in the name, since eventually there were two ruling consuls, and they were required to consult, so much so that each was empowered to annul or veto the actions of the other, especially if guided to do so by the senate. Each consul was elected to office for one year only, this ensuring that the chief executive power was shared around among the magnates. They were assisted by ranks of lower offices, governors, treasurers, public works officials and generals when the need arose. Each office was regarded as a high honour, and the word *honos* actually became a synonym for office of state. The ranks of offices were conceived of as a ladder, and aspiring politicians were expected to rise through the ranks of officialdom, hoping one day to achieve the consulship. When a man became consul, he was regarded as a personage of high nobility, and his family was ennobled.

The ordinary people were given a formal share in ruling with a place in the main voting assembly, but they were ranked according to wealth along the lines of the military organization, by 'centuries', and the poorest were crowded into the lowest ranked centuries, voting in order of rank. Often the issue had been decided before the lowest centuries had voted, so regularly the formal privilege of voting could not be exercised at all. The patricians had a further hold over their inferiors. They enjoyed a sophisticated network of patron-client relationships, so that the poor who worked on their vast estates, or who otherwise received favours from the rich, were expected to support the political ambitions of their patrons. This could include surrounding them with throngs of adulation when they appeared in public, and most certainly voting for them when it did come for them to vote.

None of this is to say that the common throng had no power at all. They had their own *arcana*, the secret power of modifying or withholding their contribution to military success. In any case, some of them, by exceptional entrepreneurship, hard work, profit through the spoils of war, or sheer luck, rose in status and wealth, and the most successful of them grew in economic power equal to that of the patricians. They never removed the social stigma that separated them from the patrician caste, but they came to exercise their own political power by deploying the same resources as the patricians, including organizing their own clients to support their efforts. Perhaps some identified with the poor out of whose ranks their own families had risen. In any case, there arose a stout and committed leadership among the lower orders, and a long series of struggles between the privileged and the common people became known as 'the conflict of the orders'. The events of the struggle are shady, and come down to us from a period where historiography is imprecise, since the same or similar events in the struggle came to be recorded several times. Nevertheless, the conflict came to a head in a watershed event of more certain historicity.

Towards the end of the third century B.C. the Romans were locked in a war with threatening neighbours, the Samnites. The foot soldiers had apparently had enough of the treatment they had received from their 'betters', the officers, and sometimes they were violently herded into the military draft. Some historians do not like the word 'strike' in this context, but that is in effect what the *plebs* did. They went on strike, withdrawing their labour from military service, thus threatening the safety of the state. It was more than that, in fact. The plebeians encamped on the Janiculum, a hill outside the city – the 'accursed mount' – and formed their own parallel political organization, what the historian Livy called 'a state within a state'.[72] They formed their own assembly, passed their own resolutions, and elected their own, exclusively plebeian, officers called the tribunes. There is little doubt that there was strong and effective leadership among them.

This was a genuine crisis for the patrician republic. They met emergencies by temporarily suspending the regular constitution and appointed a *dictator* with powers to meet the emergency. In 287 B.C. at the height of the conflict they elected one Quintus Hortensius, himself a plebeian, as dictator to solve the impasse, and he met the *plebs* offering astonishing concessions. He enacted the *lex Hortensia* that equated resolutions ('plebiscites') passed by the plebeians in their exclusive assembly, the *concilium plebis* as full laws of the republic. The tribunes, though never incorporated into the formal structure of the state, were acknowledged as leaders of the *plebs* and presidents of their assemblies.

For their part, the plebeians, conducting their assembly under divine authority, declared their tribunes, of whom there would eventually be ten elected every year, to be *sacrosanct*. The *plebs* swore an oath that meant the persons of the tribunes were inviolable – they would tear to pieces any who touched them in anger. It was mob rule converted into regular practice, although Cicero never forgave them for their 'sedition'. Their office gave them the power of veto against the actions of the consuls, and against enactments of the regular assemblies, and even resolutions of the senate. It was an immense power, in which the nobles quickly saw an opportunity. It stemmed from a 'right of intercession', which meant literally 'stepping in between'. Symbolically this involved the power for a tribune to step in to protect any citizen from being harassed by a magistrate. This apparently happened most regularly because of ill treatment during the military draft, but it applied to all cases of abuse.

The *lex Hortensia* annihilated any political distinctions between patricians and plebeians. Earlier enactments in the struggle meant that plebeians could become consuls – actually at least one consul every year had to be from the *plebs*, although the social distinctions well and truly remained. There was now, however, a new, combined patricio–plebeian nobility.[73]

One might infer from all of this that a democratic movement was in the air. The plebeians may well have thought so, but the nobles had other ideas. Hanna Pitkin is wrong to follow a long tradition from Machiavelli and Rousseau that the common people of Rome never aspired to rule themselves, but sought only a peaceful existence within the state.[74] The tribunes often lamented that they never acquired *imperium*, the official power to rule; that is, they were never incorporated into the regular array of offices. Various tribunes acted in what could be called a democratic tendency, seeking to alleviate the lot of the poor, but repeatedly they were opposed and frustrated by the senate, which was the core of a tight oligarchy that almost unceasingly controlled everything. The richer plebeians found fellow feeling with the patricians, and were a secure part of the oligarchy. The truth is that Rome was an oligarchy from start to finish.

Some observers, like Melleuish as we have seen, believed that the Roman republic 'transitioned' into the empire through the inability of its institutions to deal with populations of Roman citizens living remote from the city. There is some truth in this. Nevertheless, the overwhelming cause of its destruction was Rome's inability to deal fairly with its poorer citizens. At some time during the mid-second century B.C. tribunes began to lead their people into aggressive action to raise the lot of the poor. There is a historical lacuna for the period, especially with the loss of the relevant books of Livy. So the events are sketchy, but in 151 B.C. a tribune actually imprisoned a consul, an unthinkable occurrence. Something similar occurred again in 138 B.C., indicating that the plebeians were flexing their muscles, most likely again over problems with the draft. Then in 133 B.C. tribunician action began the process that unravelled the republic.

Tiberius Gracchus, of a plebeian noble family, and one educated in generous Stoic principles, was elected tribune and enacted before the plebeian assembly an agrarian law designed to redistribute public land to poor citizens. It was the custom of the wealthy nobility to occupy public lands as 'squatters' and use them for their own benefit. Gracchus's law, which restricted the use of the land by the nobles, incurred the uncontained wrath of the senate, who recruited a rival tribune to their cause and had him veto Gracchus's bill. In an unprecedented act of constitutional manipulation, Gracchus had the assembly depose the rival, Marcus Octavius, so that he could proceed with his legislation. The tribunate of Gracchus is complicated with many ramifications, but for present purposes the conflict with the senate is central. Roman magistrates were not prosecuted while in office, but they could be held to account when they left. Perhaps hoping to avoid prosecution, Gracchus again tested out the limits of established practice by standing immediately for a second tribuneship. There was an election riot, and in fury a band of senators armed with cudgels rushed upon Gracchus and bludgeoned him to death.

Whatever we think of the occurrence, ancient historians thought that the crowd had turned feral. Polybius, the Greek historian living in Rome from 168 B.C. thought that this was 'the first step in the demoralization of the people'.[75]

Henceforth Roman politics, which knew nothing of political party in the modern sense, was divided into two, almost armed, camps. The champions of the senate and the aristocracy, whom Cicero called 'the good men' (*boni homines*), bore the name *optimates*, while those who championed the ordinary people were the *populares*. Being a *populuris* did not necessarily mean that one was intent on improving the situation of the commoners, because reckless adventurers could as well see advantage in recruiting the crowds to their side in the new situation that began with the Gracchi.

We say 'Gracchi' because Tiberius Gracchus's program was followed up by his younger brother, Gaius, who was elected tribune ten years after Tiberius, in 123 B.C. Gaius had been a member of the land commission with his brother and was directly involved in the actual redistribution of the land. He continued his brother's legislative program with modifications only in the light of his experience as a land commissioner. He established the first Roman colony overseas for the settlement of the poor on land in the territory won from the conquered Carthaginians.

Since few of the urban poor at Rome were equipped for extensive travel, or still less for starting farms, Gaius planned to alleviate their plight by distributing corn at a low fixed price, the costs being subsidized by the state. As a modern apologist for the corn dole said, 'Gaius Gracchus found himself face to face with a hungry mob which was likely soon to become supreme in the state … If Rome waited too long she ran the risk of something like the Paris Commune of 1871 with a widespread Italian revolt at the same time.'[76] Again, Gaius did other things that outraged the senate. He was reputedly a powerful orator, and let slip no opportunity to denounce what senators had done to his brother.

Like Tiberius, he secured a second term of office, but his initial great popularity did not extend to a third, and his heated supporters armed themselves and staked out the Aventine Hill. The senate for the first time issued its final, or 'extreme' decree, telling the consul to do whatever it took to remove the menace. This decree was a kind of short cut taken in place of electing a dictator. It had no legal status, but gave the consul confidence that he would be immune with the support of the senators. Gaius's men were outnumbered by the force the consul raised, and he committed suicide before falling into the hands of his enemies. At least, he said, 'he had left a sword in the ribs of the Senate'.[77] Here was nothing less than 'an attempt to shift radically the distribution of power within the Roman state'.[78]

Although the Gracchi were men of high plebeian nobility, we have no reason to believe that their concern for the lot of the poor was not genuine, and at least among their followers were surely men of democratic leanings. Such intent was futile, since democracy was structurally impossible under the constitution of the Roman republic.[79] Herein lies the key to the distinction to be made so clearly between the original democracy of Greece and the original republicanism. The aristocratic establishment was so entrenched that it was inevitable that the representatives of privilege and status, the *optimates,* would fight back to the death – certainly to the death of the republic. So it was that the reforms of the Gracchi, and their ruin, 'set in train the events that culminated with the fall of the Republic'.[80] Here was the first stirring of the Roman civil wars.

Throughout the period the gap between rich and poor yawned ever wider. The magnates were in charge of the republic from the outset, but they were able to use its structures and processes, and the political privileges they enjoyed, to increase their wealth, while the misery of the poor plummeted as rapidly. The failure of the republic was less a matter of the scope of administration as its inability to deal with this problem. It could not cope with 'the violent fermentation evoked at Rome by the twin forces of plutocracy and pauperism ...'[81] A similar process is evident in the United States of today.

An obvious course for paupers to seek temporary survival was to join the army. As the civil war progressed, this could include the mercenary private forces of individual wealthy adventurers. The chaos started to take shape under the rise of one Gaius Marius, a 'new man' (*novus homo)* from Arpinum, also Cicero's home town. That is to say, he was not from the Roman aristocracy, but rose to prominence through military prowess. He ennobled his family by his election for the consulship in 109 B.C. to prosecute a war in Africa, and again in 104 B.C. against Germans in the north. He made a radical and consequential change to military organization. Whereas previously soldiers had to register on some scale of self-support, Marius enrolled the proletariat, those who could produce nothing but offspring, mainly from rural peasants impoverished by the encroachment of the rich upon their meager holdings, and finding subsistence near impossible.[82]

Because the fear of the Germans was so great, and Marius's reputation as a saviour so widespread, he was against all constitutional precedent and law successively elected to consulships between 104 and 101 B.C. 'The popular will had advanced a *parvenu* to a dignity far greater than any noble had attained.'[83] To reward his soldiers' loyalty, Marius renewed land distributions for them, a program that aroused hostility and stirred up new election riots. 'The Roman poor were now armed – and alienated from traditional patterns of behaviour, as the ready resort to violence in the years after 103 shows.'[84]

Although the successive elections of Marius were unconstitutional, his own behaviour was orderly and regular, befitting the hero that he became for the poor. Yet his new methods of recruitment, and the personal loyalty he received from his troops, was looked upon as the example for the military adventurers and bravados who came along after him. 'The Marian army reforms took a sinister turn only when a general appealed to his troops to help *him* against the Senate or the Comitia.'[85]

A lieutenant in Marius's army, Cornelius Sulla, was an equal, if not better, strategist than Marius. He was a successful general in the 'social wars' against Rome's insurgent Italian allies. Sulla was elected consul for 88 B.C., and was given command of the punitive war against Mithridates, the king of Pontus in the east, who had annexed Roman territory. He and his soldiers expected great wealth from the spoils of conquest. Planning land distributions in Italy that would disadvantage the aristocracy, Sulla was replaced by the senate, which gave the eastern command to Marius.

In revenge Sulla turned his troops against the city of Rome, 'to the undying infamy of his name', as they said in the film, *Spartacus.* The city was circumscribed by a sacred boundary, the pomoerium. The area of the city within the pomoerium was strictly civilian territory, and generals on active command, and armies, were not permitted to cross it. The exception was when a conquering army was accorded a triumph by law, and they were welcomed into the city with acclaim. The supreme assembly of the state, the *comitia centuriata,* was constituted on military lines, and met outside the pomoerium. Sulla's invasion was both sacrilege and treason. Yet force of arms prevailed and Sulla moved to eliminate all his political enemies by posting up proscription lists labelling them outlaws.

As opposed to his rival Marius, who escaped the persecution, Sulla was on the side of the aristocracy, an extreme optimate. He abolished the corn dole and moved to curtail the powers of the tribunate, legislating that all laws be taken to the *comitia centuriata*, not the assembly of the *plebs*, and then only after senatorial approval had been acquired. He took up the eastern command again, but returned to Rome in 83 B.C. and had himself declared dictator, an office that had long fallen into disuse. He dispensed with the formal time limit for the dictatorship, claiming the office and its extraordinary powers without limit. He now had all the powers and honours of a king without adopting the hated word itself.[86] With a king in all but name, the *res publica* survived only as a memory. After Sulla the old constitution had been fatally damaged, and he had entrenched 'the vicious nexus between an army and its commander'.[87]

With Sulla's lawless adventure as precedent, and the fact that he got away with it despite all the republican laws supposed to ensure the stability of the state, the field was open slather. We do not have scope to trace the fortunes of the dominant men during the turbulent days of the republic in its death throes. Pompey, Crassus, Octavian, Lepidus, Mark Antony, and most ominously Julius Caesar had their eyes on claiming the state. The orator, philosopher, and statesman, Cicero also had his turn at rule, being consul in 63 B.C., but he remained the leading defender of evanescent republican ideals. Yet his notion of 'the people's affair' had little to do with engaging the people in the enterprise of governing the state. His term of office also experienced an outbreak of violence.

The final years of the republic were so chaotic that it is difficult to identify any particular turning point. Obviously, however, the career and downfall of Caesar was both a culmination of constitutional dissolution and a giant step on the path to the ruin of the republic. Caesar was born into a high patrician family of ancient lineage, but chose a populist route to dominance.[88] Like the other 'great men' he was an outstanding soldier and general. Although a patrician, he was also a nephew of Marius, and enjoyed the support of his uncle's veterans. Combining this with a liberal program of bribery, he became high priest of the republic at a young age, bringing him directly into political contention. Being able to declare bad omens at critical times, the *pontifex maximus* had much influence over public affairs. And he may have been, as some claim, the greatest general in history.

For political convenience Caesar formed a coalition with two rival generals, Pompey and Crassus, which became known as 'the first triumvirate', although there was nothing constitutional in their arrangement. Caesar was elected consul in 59 B.C. and was given the command against the Gauls in the north. He first conducted land distributions to the poor, acting illegally by using troops to intimidate opponents. His Gallic wars kept him away from Rome for nine years, but he was perturbed by news of the success of his rivals at home. In straightforward, unemotional prose, he wrote a detailed account for posterity of his successive military victories, which included several acts of genocide.

In 49 B.C. Caesar stood for the consulship in absentia. A person could not be tried while holding office, and his candidature may have been a ploy to avoid prosecution for his actions during his previous consulship. The senate opposed him, and issued its 'final', emergency decree against him. With his customary decisiveness (or recklessness) he trusted to Fortuna and crossed the Rubicon river marking the border between his province and Italy. This was high treason, and the optimates organized a defensive force against him, under Pompey as general. Yet Caesar was a popular hero everywhere he went, and the infamous memory of Sulla was no deterrent to his success. He was received in Rome with popular adoration, and the republican army withdrew from Italy to Greece to wait out his success.

Caesar pursued them and in August 48 B.C. engaged the republicans' much larger force, outmanoeuvering Pompey's hesitant command. Caesar began his legendary affair with Cleopatra in Egypt, but in Rome he was given every honour under the sun.

He was elected to successive consulships, and in 46 B.C. he was made dictator for ten years and in 44 he was made dictator for life. With supreme but unrecognized irony he was made 'prefect of public morals' for life, while public figures were sworn to obey him and protect his person. The ugly word 'king' raised its head, while he himself was alleged to have thought that the term 'republic' was an empty cipher.[89]

Caesar rose to power as a populist, a *popularis* claiming to be the saviour of the people. He was generous with his own vast riches when they were needed to buy support, but in supreme power he turned open contempt on all the traditions of the republic, depriving the people of their voting rights and dismissing the tribunes when they displeased him.[90] The oath of protection did not work, and in March 44 B.C. some sixty disaffected politicians conspired to do away with him *to save the republic*. Yet the old constitution had been destroyed irreparably. Caesar had named his great nephew, Marcus Octavius, his heir, bestowing the name of Caesar Octavian. The precedent of a triple coalition was followed, and Octavian teamed up with Mark Antony and Caesar's Master of the Horse (the deputy to the dictator), Lepidus, as the 'second triumvirate'.

They too were given dictatorial powers with the explicit commission to *reconstitute the republic*, no less. They launched a savage program of proscriptions against Caesar's murderers and all their other enemies; Cicero, not actually a conspirator, but a sworn enemy of Antony, fell to an assassin's sword. The armies of the chief conspirators against Caesar, Brutus and Cassius, were holed up at Philippi, and there they were defeated by Octavian and Antony in 42 B.C. The nineteen-year-old heir of Caesar, Octavian, demanded to be made consul, and like his adoptive father marched on Rome when he did not immediately get his way.

The triumvirate was renewed in 37 B.C. but of course as ambitious men they fell out. Lepidus rather faded from prominence and Antony courted Caesar's old mistress, Cleopatra in Egypt. They married that same year and Octavian's propaganda spread the word that the couple were planning to annex Rome to Egypt. He turned on them and they engaged in battle at Actium in northern Greece in 31 B.C. Antony and Cleopatra were defeated and Octavian was the last of the adventurers still standing. He was now the undisputed master of the Roman world 'which had been his unwavering ambition through fourteen years of civil war. To this end, he had been responsible for death, destruction, confiscation, and unbroken misery on a scale quite unmatched in all the previous phases of Roman civil conflict over the past century ...'[91] For all that, he adopted a style draped in sanctity, 'Augustus', and although he claimed his position to be '*princeps*' 'first citizen', he had become the emperor.

The Republican
Legacy of Rome

The foregoing account would seem to show that the republic simply fell to the ambitions of powerful rivals. The point, however, is that institutions supposedly designed to protect the public were inadequate to the task. The institutional structure of republican Rome was complex, and need not detain us here. Nevertheless, there were certain implicitly republican tendencies in the structures, surrounded by a stout ideology in defence of republican ideals.

The republican legacy falls under three broad categories: the role of virtue, the place of the 'mixed constitution', and the aversion to change. While my account rejects any idea that republicanism begins with the Greeks, and holds that republicanism was a Roman invention, many of the lines of Roman thought were borrowed from the Greeks, or were adaptations of ideas that had arisen among the Greeks.

First, virtue. This was the republican ideal that resonated with Machiavelli, the Christian 'commonwealth' of the English interregnum, the French committee of public safety, and particularly with the American founders. It corresponded with the Greek *aretê*, which meant excellence, moral goodness, and in Homer manliness, strength in battle. From Aristotle the Romans gleaned a passion for virtue, which he had conceived of as a 'divine Form', and lyricized in his poetry. His view was a far cry from Homer's, since *aretê* for Aristotle represented something like the virtue of a chaste maiden. Virtue creates the good polity, in which true happiness can be achieved by allowing all persons to develop their full human potential.

The Latin term *virtus* sounded more like the Homeric version, because it derived from the gendered term for man, *vir*. Its first meaning was manliness, manhood. Roman aristocrats were often educated in Stoic philosophy, where virtue was a central concept. The eclectic Cicero thought that virtue meant to live modestly according to nature and 'nature's law'.[92] The Stoics held that virtue came in four species: wisdom, courage, justice and temperance. A person who embodied these was a 'wise man', who did not allow passion of any kind to overcome him. A 'wise man', accepting the natural order to be produced by divine goodness, could take everything that came to him with equanimity. He could endure pain, deprivation, abuse, as external things indifferent to his essential being.

Cicero thought that virtue thus produced the ideal statesman, the kind that led Rome to its prominence in the world, and it certainly included military prowess. In his attempt to redirect Rome onto a genuinely republican course during the troubles of its last years, Cicero held up the second century Roman statesman, Publius Cornelius Scipio Aemilianus, as the model statesman, and if one such could be found he might control the passions of the military adventurers as *rector rei publicae*, a kind of guide of the republic. Virtue built the republic, and Rome bequeathed virtue to the world.

Studying the founding years of the Roman republic, Machiavelli was impressed by virtue. Under his pen virtue took the manliness aspect even further than the Romans. A ruler should embrace virtue and let fortune, or fate, contingency, go hang. He characterized fortune as a raging river in flood, which must be tamed with levees and earthworks. Alternatively, fortune was a fickle temptress who must be taken firmly in hand and dominated. A powerful ruler exercises *virtù* by doing whatever it takes to maintain his estate, since stability against all disruptive forces is paramount.

Second, the mixed constitution. The Greek philosophers, probably starting with Plato, especially in his *Statesman (Politicus)*, had a penchant for classifying the constitutions of states according to the way in which they were ruled. The simplest classification was rule by the one, the few, and the many. It was then clear that a moral dimension was needed and that there were good versions of all three, and corresponding bad versions. Aristotle arranged them into their counterparts, which implied that one could degenerate into its opposite. Aristotle followed Plato in thinking that the rule of one completely virtuous person was the most efficient and the most virtuous state – a monarchy; if you could not have this, then rule by a few excellent men was the next best – aristocracy; and if you must have it, rule by the many according to nature and nature's law was an acceptable form of government – polity. Yet rule by one bad man would be a tyranny, a few such, oligarchy, and by an unruly mob, democracy!

Aristotle thought that the 'middle class' were more virtuous than the avid super-rich who were hungry for self-aggrandizement, and the poor, who threatened the state because they could not endure their deprivations. A state built on a strong, stable middle class could contain the excesses of the rich and the poor. The Greek historian, Polybius, who had been brought to Rome captive after the defeat of the Greeks at Pydna in 168 B.C., was welcomed into the top circles of the Roman aristocracy on account of his high culture and his interest in the pursuits of warfare. He became a great admirer of Rome, and searched for the causes of Rome's greatness. In the sixth book of his history he set out to analyse the republican constitution, which he thought to be a deciding factor in Rome's success. Polybius was of course steeped in the philosophy of his homeland, and was influenced by Aristotle's classification of constitutions.

His own contribution was the *anacyclosis* – a never ending cycle through the various forms of constitution. Monarchy was the best (most natural) form of government, but power was apt to corrupt and the king would be tempted into tyrannical ways. Then a few good men would oust the tyrant and establish an aristocracy, but they too would fall to greed, and degenerate into an oligarchy; in which event the people would rise up and establish the rule of the many. In time the people would overreach themselves, become unruly and degenerate into anarchy or mob rule, which Polybius called *ochlocracy*. The situation would then be rescued by a powerful good man, who would establish a monarchy. And so on.

The constant deterioration was intolerable, but inevitable. The best that could be hoped for was that sound constitutional arrangements would hold the line for stability, at least for a time. At the high point of the republic, and during Rome's rapid expansion into an empire ruled by a republic, Polybius thought that Rome had solved the problem. The way to arrest the cycle of constitutions was to mix all three good forms, rule by the one, the few and the many, and indeed, he contended, the Roman republic had done just that.

It was all a piece of abstract sophistry. That Rome had mixed the 'pure' forms was sheer fantasy. First, Polybius said that Rome had a monarchic 'part' in the consulship. All government requires an executive function, but to call the consulship monarchic was a fundamental distortion. The consulship was intended to annihilate the idea of kingship – there being two consuls required to consult, who were in office for one year without re-election. In the senate Polybius rightly discerned the rule of the few. It was composed of aristocrats, or 'nobles' in the combined patricio–plebeian nobility, but it acted at all times as an *oligarchy*, what Aristotle characterized as the rule of wealth. The people were marginally involved in government through the major assemblies, and as we have seen, asserted themselves in the *concilium plebis*, the people's self-help assembly, but Rome was nowhere near to the democracy that Polybius claimed its constitution embraced.

Polybius inherited from his Greek philosophical forebears an obsession with stability, or resistance to change. His renaissance follower, Machiavelli, thought time was an insidious enemy.[93] In any case Polybius had imputed to the Roman constitution a deep conservatism, which is the third of the important legacies Rome left to republican theory. His contribution was 'a typical product of Greek political speculation in that it identified perfection with immobility and saw political evolution as the road to disorder and ruin'.[94] In the literary panegyrics of Livy and Vergil, the principate of Augustus was the very institution designed to thwart further change and arrest the decline into moral degeneration.

Cicero, forever associated with the defence of republican ideals, was aghast at the actual changes in Rome's governmental system, and abhorred the instability that was the reality during his day. He had great faith in the senate, filled as it was by men of property, and property was the ground of economic and social stability. Yet, he said, 'In such a large number of citizens there is a big crowd of those who out of fear of punishment and conscious of their own crimes, seek revolution and changes in the form of the republic, or who, because of an inbuilt disaffection, feed on civil discord and insurrection, or who, because of family entanglements would rather have the neighbourhood ablaze than get burnt themselves.'[95]

A witness to the chaos of the 50s of the last century of the republic, Cicero was horrified at the faction-riven aristocracy, divided between the *optimates* and the *populares*. Even a *popularis* could be on the side of the good if he was acting to defend the constitution. But the root cause of the troubles was the exclusion of the ordinary people from proper consideration: '… high prices, infertility of the fields, poor harvests. *Hunger was the background of the constant violence of the 50s,* perhaps more often than we know.'[96] Yet the *optimates'* position was that nothing should change and erode their privilege. 'The retort of the conservative politician was the retort of Maître Pangloss, an assurance to the proletariat that all was for the best in the best of all possible worlds.'[97]

Cicero wrote his treatise 'On the republic', *De Re Publica*, in defence of republican ideals. He concurred in Polybius's belief

48

that Rome was the ideal state, as long as the senate remained firmly in charge. He had no illusions about democracy. The liberty of 'the people' was to submit themselves to the rule of the senate. As for the people's self-help office, the tribunate, it was born in sedition for the purposes of revolution.[98] To Cicero the tribunate and the popular assembly were at the root of instability.

In short, the republic as 'the people's business' was a fiction. The mixed constitution, and checks and balances, were deeply conservative devices, dreamed up in the defence of the status quo, and that meant in defence of the entrenched privilege of wealth. The failure actually to include the people in the constitution in any meaningful way, and the chronic neglect of their desperate needs, their pauperism, radicalized them not into a concerted popular revolution, but enlisted them to seek fortune with the wealthy and ever greedy magnates. The republic was from its origins to its destruction the affair of the wealthy and ambitious, and the people in effect had no part in it.

The Republic
of the United States

One may reasonably ask, what has Rome to do with America? Little indeed before the War of Independence and the appearance of the republican constitution after the chaos of war. Yet the founders of the United States, those who wrote the constitution, were almost to a man highly educated, and many of them were fine classicists, intimate with Roman history. They also knew Greek history, and as much as they admired Rome and its empire so they despised Athens and its populist culture. We must reach beyond the external trappings of Roman influence – the senate, the capitol, the electoral 'college', the classical architecture, the sculptures and frescoes. There were home-grown reasons for this revulsion. Before the war against British rule, there was a strong build-up of an urge for freedom, a 'contagion of liberty'.[99]

To begin with, the American colonies arguably furnished us with the first early modern version of democracy since ancient Athens. The colony of Massachusetts was founded by migrating Calvinists from the old country, where they believed they had been persecuted. It was a religious dispute, these 'puritans' believing that the national church in England had not pursued the purifications required by the reformation far enough. Many 'popish' hangovers persisted in the Church of England, and those who wished to change them were persecuted by church and state together. The oppression by Charles I ended in civil war, pursued on the parliamentary side by Presbyterians and Independents (the name adopted by the puritans).

The Independents hived off into separate congregations, wherein all business was conducted by the communicants themselves. There was a part precedent for the way they governed themselves in the methods of the Anglican parish councils, but in the Independents' case there was no supervision from bishops, priests or elders. When persecution got too much for them, some congregations emigrated and sought shelter in the protestant Netherlands. The Massachusetts founders looked for freedom in the new world, which they regarded as *terra nullius*. Stephen Fry has pronounced that they did not migrate for freedom, but so that they themselves could persecute. Herein lies the controversy with the puritans. They indeed dealt shamefully with those they regarded as heretics, and in their own intransigence they indirectly produced a truly free colony when Roger Williams seceded to found Rhode Island.

What we are concerned with here, however, is the democratic mode of government. When they landed on 'virgin' territory, the Independents had to build not just a church, but also a community, from scratch. This included town planning, public building works, roads and bridges, public finances, dealings with the 'natives' and other settlements and trade with the old world. Their concerns extended to the welfare of their residents. Before they landed, their leader, John Winthrop, preached a shipboard sermon that might have overjoyed Aristotle, because he urged his community to live together as friends, in love and peace with one another. In a ringing phrase, he urged them to 'abridge themselves of their superfluities', live simple lives and give their 'superfluities' to the poor and needy.[100]

In making their communal decisions, they acted as a congregation. The way they conducted church affairs was the way they organized and built their settlement, with every member taking part in debate over the decisions and owning the outcomes. The comparison with Athenian democracy was apparent to some, because their leaders were asked to reflect on the matter, and one pastor, the former parish priest of Boston in Lincolnshire, John Cotton, said there was a big difference between the decision making of ancient pagans and those under the direction of the holy spirit. On another occasion, he conceded that their method of self-government was close to what prevailed in Athens.[101]

The New England town meeting persists to this day, but it is scarcely more than a reminder of genuinely democratic days, confined as it now is to local affairs in a monster nation-state. Old New England itself eventually succumbed to the American dream of acquiring riches through industry and trade, and the early experiment was almost the last we learn of true institutional democracy in America.

Nevertheless, the settlements of north America spread into thirteen separate colonies, while a growing dissatisfaction with remote British rule aroused strong resentment, a desire for self-government, and the raging 'contagion' of liberty. The immigrant population began to feel that they were being persecuted by British rule, under which they were taxed without representation. The many grievances the colonists had with their rulers need not detain us here. A revolutionary war was fought against the British crown with remarkable, and unexpected success. The leader, George Washington, was America's first super-hero.

With the war won, the separate colonies formed their own autonomous constitutions. Ordinary men, 'backwoodsmen', who had fought in the war were filled with a new confidence, and crowded into the newly independent legislatures. The war had left many in serious debt, mainly to the wealthy traders and magnates of the eastern seaboard, and the new legislators were in a mood to flex their muscles against their tormentors. There was much radical legislation, including the disestablishment of the church, redistribution of public lands to the poor, issuing of paper money, which relieved many who had to repay debts. In Boston a newspaper complained that 'sedition itself' was legislating.[102] In Massachusetts an armed rebellion of impoverished famers challenged the government because the legislature there had refused to issue paper money.

The war of independence had been conducted under a loose confederation of the thirteen rebelling colonies, which sent delegates to confer on the course of action. This arrangement was powerless to assist the colonies with their various post-war troubles, and leading men began to talk of centralized government and nation-building. Among the elites of society, it was the unruly nature of the assemblies, and the arrogance of upstart politicians, that spurred them into seeking a new constitution. A group of businessmen met at Annapolis in 1786 to urge the Continental Congress to authorize a convention to consider ways of facilitating commercial cooperation among the states, and 'other matters'. The commission to the convention that met at Philadelphia in 1787 was 'for the sole and express purpose of revising the Articles of Confederation'. Since several delegates turned up with new draft constitutions in their pockets, it was evident that there was a nationalist mood abroad. The convention acted *ultra vires*, and the foundations of the new constitution were in fact illegal.

Even American writers who criticize the constitution that was produced at Philadelphia in 1787 temper their severity with mandatory homage to the founders: the fifty-five were all men of genius, true representatives of the enlightenment, men of unmatched skill, and never before or since in history was such a collection of talent gathered together in one place for a common purpose. They themselves learnt from Machiavelli that fortune was a tide to be taken at the flood, and the occasion of their gathering was a high point in history. The other metaphor that occurred to them was that fortune was a wheel, and men situated at the high point of its turning must take steps somehow to arrest the decline.[103] They believed that the 'mixed constitution' as formulated by Polybius was the answer to their problem. The constitution that they should frame should stand against the downturn of the wheel, and keep the inevitable blackguards who would seek power for evil purposes out of the system. They thought that their invention was 'the culmination of western civilization', but its idealization did not take into account the radical *novum* of federalism and the written, static constitution.[104]

In the temper of the times persons who sought power were never up to any good. They drew from Bolingbroke's stand against Walpole in England that the ways of government were inevitably evil, that power was always corrupting, and that to be in opposition to government was more moral than to govern. There was little room for good men to consult the public interest in the deployment of political power, at least among those who would come hereafter. From the widely read 'Cato's letters', penned in England by Trenchard and Gordon who echoed Machiavelli's pessimism about human nature, they learnt that people seeking power were never to be trusted, and that strong defences should be erected to contain and exclude them.[105] The constitution was to be deliberately designed to be static, conservative.

The delegates were also men of wealth and substance, of high education and social standing. Concerning the defence of the constitution, in *The Federalist*, written by James Madison, John Jay and Alexander Hamilton, '… every fundamental appeal in it is to some material and substantial interest.' Above all, it was directed to owners of property 'anxious to find a foil against the attacks of leveling democracy'.[106] It is true that Charles Beard, who made these comments, has been heavily attacked by republicans, but the truth of his criticism is evident in almost every aspect of United States history.

The Federalist, circulated to encourage endorsement among the colonies, made it clear that one of the chief purposes of the constitution had been to contain the licence of ordinary persons. Democracy was a target, and James Madison, the chief drafter of the constitution, declared that republicanism and democracy were far apart, and that one of the functions of the republic was to exclude the possibility of democracy.[107] In the debates several of the founders denounced democracy as infected with 'disease', 'turbulence' and 'folly'. The man who would become the second president of the United States, John Adams, was sure that the constitution was a defence of property, and that it was among men of property that virtue truly resided. In fact, the lack of property was the root cause of vice, since irrational desire 'inflamed [the landless] with ambition and avarice'.[108] It is truly curious that the Constitution of the United States is now so vigorously promoted as the defence of democracy.

The Mixed Constitution

As has been noted, Machiavelli and before him Polybius were serious influences on the founders of the United States. These believed that they would preserve the new union and defend it against the turning tide of corrupt politicians by writing a constitution that could not easily be changed, and that deployed mechanisms for ensuring that concerted power could not be exercised. This was the principle of checks-and-balances. Madison expressed an inordinate fear of factions, which many thought were the cause of instability in a state. Alexander Hamilton likened them to 'convulsions'.[109] The Romans had attempted to check power by forming the magistrates into 'colleges', where each officer could check and veto the others. Madison was devoted to the dispersal of power to prevent 'factions' gaining control, and significantly, the faction that he most feared was the faction of 'the multitude'. Again, what price the *res publica* of the model republic?

The Americans, influenced by Montesquieu's misconstruction of the British constitution, adopted a system of separated powers.[110] The chief organs of government were set off against each other: Congress (the legislature) against the Presidency (the executive), and the Supreme Court (the judiciary) against both. Any 'faction' or political adventurer getting hold of one of these centres of power should be obstructed by the other two. The federal system, invented by the Americans as a unified national government, ensured also that the states hold a measure of power against the federal government and against each other. Separation both exalted and diminished the office of president. The president took the place of a king, and had to appear as the unifying focus of the nation, but he [maybe she] was also a political leader, who in some circumstances might face a completely hostile congress. In that case a president would have to cajole and pander to the congressmen and women to beg support for both policies and legislation. Often this included 'logrolling', using the power of presidential finances to provide benefits for the constituencies of biddable congressmen. John Adams exulted in that he could count eight layers of obstacle to the pursuit of power.

Thomas Jefferson, who was aware that the constitution had strong anti-democratic tendencies, thought that change was necessary. There could be scarcely a more blatant provision for the distancing of the people from the levers of power than the electoral college for choosing the president, when it was believed that only men of substance were wise enough to make the right choice. Moreover, the constitution contrived to count black slaves in the population as the equivalent of two-thirds of a full citizen. This may have been an expedient device to limit the claims to representative power on the part of southern slaveholders, but it tacitly impugned the humanity of large sections of the inhabitants, when the *Declaration of Independence* had declared all to be created equal. In any case, the constitution was made highly difficult to amend, requiring concurrent majorities of the nation and in three quarters of the states.

Jefferson was not himself a member of the constitutional convention, he being representative to the government of France at the time, but he wrote to Madison proposing that the constitution be rewritten and updated every ten years in order to move with the times. Madison replied that it would be dangerous to excite the 'passions' of the people so frequently.[111]

In summary, the founding of the Constitution of the United States invoked three basic principles drawn from historical example and philosophical reflection. First, the constitution embodied virtue. We have seen that among the Romans *virtus* embraced the characteristics of the warrior statesman: strength, courage, determination, endurance, and above all, 'manliness'. Panegyricists like Cicero and Livy could invoke these virtues as the cause of Rome's rise to greatness. Machiavelli, studying Rome in detail, modified his *virtù* to mean whatever it takes to subdue the vagaries of fortune and to maintain a stable order by ruthless imposition of the will. Machiavelli repudiated the Christianity of his day for inducing meekness,[112] but the Americans were much formed by Christian belief. From John Locke they imbibed a sense of the purposes of nature and nature's God, under whom their constitution should be a contract among God's created people. They therefore took virtue seriously as a moral undertaking, and were comforted by Locke's assurance that the accumulation of property was itself a virtuous undertaking.[113] Perhaps the republicans were induced to pay little heed to the repeated injunctions of the gospels to bring justice to the poor.

Second, the constitution should resist change, particularly democratic progress. Institutionally, the mixed constitution was theorized to postpone change as long as possible. The view of morality reflected by the constitution was individualist. A baron of industry could accumulate great wealth, and in conscience could redistribute his accumulations through private charity, of which there is a long tradition in America. The bias against collective welfare action runs deep. Harvey Mansfield Jr insists that government has no moral purpose, but that it exists merely to keep the community afloat. Yet even that negative, highly conservative, approach breaks down when large sections of the community, as of now and also as in the aftermath of the War of Independence, are deprived of the basic means of a tolerable life. The existence of a 'working poor' is a terrible indictment on the United States' constitutional set-up. To say nothing of the unemployed, the sick, the disabled, the forcibly dispossessed and homeless.

The proponents of liberalism project economic individualism deeply into the American character. Democracy vacated the field of politics and entered the economic realm. Daniel Boorstin saw that the immigration of Europe's poor into the new world transformed them into economic activists intent on building up their own security through wealth. American democracy was embedded in 'the attainment of wealth', and, failing that, at least 'reaching for it'.[114] Joyce Appleby went a little further. Immigration to America brought about nothing less than a *redefinition of human nature*. Prosperity caused the 'democratization' of economic life. For her the constitution was not a reaction against post-revolutionary democracy, but the creation of a national market. Democracy became an economic category rather than a political one. 'Democratic values were invoked not to enlarge the people's power in government but rather to justify the abandonment of the authority traditionally exercised over them.'[115] The removal of democracy from the republican order was complete.

Subsequent American theorists of democracy redesigned the concept to fit the American economic order. Realist definitions saw clearly that the United States was ruled by elites, not by the people, whose role was reduced to judge between competing elites.[116] The iron law of oligarchy held firm. Numerous empirical studies then informed us that people without property included many with personality defects, prone to disorder and violence; best to keep the 'ordinary' out of politics, and where the many were 'ignorant and apathetic' it was functional to let sleeping dogs lie.[117]

Thirdly, therefore, the constitutional set-up of the United States was institutionally conservative. Since conservatism is a time-honoured political creed, its embedding in the *institutions* of government more-or-less permanently ruled out competing ideologies. Marxism became public enemy number one, and the subject of public witch-hunts, while socialism – even democratic socialism, *pace* Bernie Sanders – was virtually banned from public discourse. At least mention of it usually met gales of ridicule, if not angry ululation.

Combatting Democracy

Despite what has been said here about the anti-democratic tenor of the founding, Americans have laid claim to a species called 'Madisonian democracy'. Madison harboured deep fears about the damage to be caused by 'faction'. In his pessimistic view of human nature, infected by innate greed and selfishness, factions were inevitable. Yet to suppress faction by the organs of government would be to deny people their rights and to crush their liberties. While abhorring faction, he recognized 'interests' among the people, which guaranteed the dispersal of power among various groups. At this point his politics meshes with the economic interpretation of democracy. Yet it should be remembered that a plurality of associations is a prerequisite and a condition of any truly democratic polity. It is unfortunate in the extreme that Madison was not able to connect more directly the 'interests' of the people with the conduct of their government. His pluralism was in reality a defence against institutional democracy.

The continuing story of American democracy is one of struggle with a republican set-up that privileged wealth, connected wealth to political power, and rendered collective action on the part of, or on behalf of, the people, not only undesirable but also nigh impossible.

Jefferson was the first real hero of the democratic struggle. He was reluctant vice-president to the second president of the United States, John Adams. As we could have inferred from his strident writings, Adams was a severe advocate of central power, as long as it was in the right hands. Many Democratic-Republican associations devoted to the constitution's dispersal of power antagonized Adams. Reacting to the spate of journalism denouncing his authoritarianism, Adams sponsored a Sedition Act that was aimed at silencing opposition. Jefferson called his narrow victory over Adams at the presidential election 'the revolution of 1800', 'as real a revolution in the principles of our government as that of 1776 was in its form'.[118] At his inaugural Jefferson announced qualified support for the constitution's containment of popular passion: 'though the will of the majority is in all cases to prevail, that will to be rightful must be reasonable'.[119] Among Jefferson's achievements as president was to encourage people of humble origin to enter high office. He engendered a ferment of democratic fervour through his repudiation of federalist elitism.

Jefferson's struggle for democracy centred on opposition to the chief financial interests. In 1791 the secretary of the treasury, Alexander Hamilton, sponsored the establishment of the first National Bank of America. This was to be a private institution under the supervision of the federal government. Jefferson, and his Virginia friends, James Madison and John Randolph, argued that it was unconstitutional for the government to be involved since it was encroaching on states' residual rights. Jefferson's chief objection to the bank was that it became a centre of privilege and the power of wealth. It was an 'aristocratic engine',[120] and in its various guises became the institutional focus of the financial hegemony that would forever hold the fledgling democracy of the republican-democrat's hostage.

The democratic spirit sponsored by Jefferson's leadership broke out in great fervour with the anti-slavery movement. It was genuinely democratic because it rested upon belief in the equality of humankind. The lead was taken by the growing numbers of Quakers, supported in throngs by Methodists and Baptists. The second great religious revival, spreading from Yale University around the turn of the nineteenth century, helped to reunify the nation, bitterly divided in its diversity, particularly because of the scourge of slave ownership. One of the Yale leaders of the movement, Lyman Beecher, held that Christianity had become the cement of society, supplying 'the deficiency of political affinity and interest.'[121] What was religious was also political, creating 'the institutional basis of what would become an entirely new kind of political power, democratic in tone and sophisticated in its organizational tactics, but different from the main forms of democratic politics that had emerged since the Revolution'.[122]

Jefferson had been successful in organizing groups in his support, and he was skilful in managing Congress. His friend and successor, Madison, though of subtle mind, lacked Jefferson's organizing skills, and neither he nor his successors, James Monroe and John Quincy Adams, son of the second president, were capable of mobilizing the presidency in active support for the people's benefit. Yet the Jeffersonian spirit was still abroad when a new champion arose, the victor over the British at New Orleans, Andrew Jackson. Leading the Republican-Democrats, Jackson was elected to the presidency in 1828. He was determined to use his power for the benefit of ordinary people, and in particular to thwart the ambitions of the privileged, the 'extractors', 'an unproductive class of bankers, speculators, and their ilk [who] lived luxuriously by reason of its privileged position in a complex politico-economic system symbolized by the Monster Bank'.[123]

> ... when the law undertakes to add to these natural and just advantages artificial distinctions, to grand titles, gratuities and exclusive privileges, to make the rich richer and the potent more powerful, the humble members of society – the farmers, mechanics and laborers – who have neither the time nor the means of securing like favors to themselves, have a right to complain of the injustice of their Government.[124]

To Jackson the true virtue of the republic resided not in the owners of wealth and property but among the 'producers' through their labour. This was a 'more hard-headed and determined version of Jeffersonian democracy'.[125]

The National Bank's twenty-year charter expired in 1811, but it was replaced in 1816 by the Second National Bank of America. Its charter of renewal came up in Jackson's presidency, but Jackson vetoed it as the bastion of privilege and 'extraction'. His protracted struggle with the bank's president, Nicholas Biddle, was a surrogate for a war between rich and poor. His rather more subtle reason for veto was that the bank, being a private company with national power levers, could fall into the hands of foreign capital and be used in traitorous ways in wartime. Jackson challenged the idea that Congress was the true representative of the American people. He was the only officer in the land who had been elected by the whole people (an excusable sophistry given the nature of the electoral college), and he justified his use of the president's veto as an example of the power of the people.[126]

The democratic temper of his rule was dramatized during Jackson's inaugural for his second term of office. The Washington establishment was shocked and outraged at the tag-rag throng who crammed the city – people of 'the lower sort', a thick slice of 'the propertyless masses'.[127] 'KING MOB' now ruled.[128] For his second term election Jackson had activated Madison's strict separation of democracy and republicanism by dropping the tag 'Republic' from his party's name – now true democrats.

Apart from the slave owning, that is. It is a great puzzle that the champions of equality, Jefferson and Jackson, were both slaveholders. Jefferson was obviously ill at ease about his equivocation between the *Declaration of Independence*, largely produced under his pen, and his own lifestyle. Yet he feared the slaughter of retribution that might break out should all the slaves be emancipated at a stroke. Abraham Lincoln was deeply hostile to the institution of slavery, and took the *Declaration of Independence* seriously. His political antennae were sensitized in reaction to the Kansas-Nebraska act and the Dred Scott court case which together implied that there was no place in the United States that was slave free.

Lincoln became leader of the newly formed Republican party, which lined up against the Jackson party that had dropped the name 'Republican'. He railed against the 'house divided', which he knew his country had become. He invested the nation with a high moral purpose derived from the *Declaration*. He therefore alienated many of the moral crusaders who believed that his campaign should be an all-out assault on slavery. Subtle politician as he was, he turned his attentions to the unity of the nation rather than the emancipation of the slaves. Yet the southern plantation owners knew well his anti-slavery disposition, and within a month of his election to the presidency in 1860, before he actually took up office, Georgia, Alabama, Mississippi, Florida and Louisiana left the Union, with Texas and others following.

Lincoln pursued the civil war in defence of the Union, and it was a war power that he invoked when in September 1862 he proclaimed that from the beginning of the following year all enslaved people in the rebel states 'shall be then, thenceforward, and forever free'. Considering the democratic ideal of human equality, this moment was the most decisive commitment to democracy in American history. As Cornell West declared, 'Lincoln exemplifies the integrity of democratic energy'.[129] This generous commitment to democracy, however, did not at all mean that the United States actually embodied a real democracy. Freedom for the emancipated slaves was elusive, because vicious discrimination against people of African descent denied them the fruits of democracy, which are still only won back piecemeal, as with the well-intentioned legislation of John F. Kennedy and Lyndon B. Johnson.

Yet it is not only black people who suffer from the static republic and stunted democracy that is the United States. Presidents Woodrow Wilson and Franklin D. Roosevelt were keenly aware of the restrictions the constitution placed upon them in the exercise of the 'power of the people'. In Roosevelt's day the philosopher and theologian, Reinhold Niebuhr, recognized that 'plutocratic [so-called] idealism' had become a 'screen for injustice'.[130] Roosevelt, like Jackson, regarded the presidency as an instrument for the collective benefit of the people, but he was attacked by conservative critics as the sinister champion of big government. Ronald Reagan, the one who announced to the world that 'government is the problem', sought to taint his memory in the nineteen-eighties by pinning on him the undeserved attribute of 'veiled socialism'.[131] Critics from the von Mises school of thought actually called him 'fascist'. Yet Roosevelt was no socialist, but a civilizer of capitalism. His commitment to the freedom and welfare of the people at large scarcely qualified him as a fascist, either, but these were dangerous sorts of comments to apply to a struggling democrat in the era of Hitler and the devastating world depression.

The present generation of neo-liberals is hell bent on dismantling his legacy and defaming Roosevelt's name. We have not the space to trace the intricacies of his extended presidency, but suffice it to say that he tried to use the presidency to relieve people's suffering and create employment during the great depression and to prosecute the war against the Nazis. John Maynard Keynes urged Roosevelt to spend public monies to stimulate growth, even though Keynes was critical of the National Recovery Act.[132] Roosevelt enjoyed huge popular support. His massive state intervention in the ailing economy met the fury of those from similarly privileged backgrounds to his own, labelling him a class traitor. The conservative Supreme Court virtually waged war against his presidency. 'Never before had the Supreme Court worked such havoc with a legislative program as it did in 1935 and 1936 with that of the New Deal nor in so short a time invalidated so many acts of Congress.'[133]

Roosevelt was genuinely devoted to democracy, but he himself tended towards the heavily inculcated American view of democracy as the province of the individual person: 'The freedoms that we must and will protect in the United States are the freedoms which will make the individual paramount in a true democracy. In our American way of life political and economic freedom go hand in hand.'[134] Nevertheless, at his second inaugural he explicitly rejected the American republican tradition that government power was a bad thing: 'The essential democracy of our Nation and the safety of our people depend not upon the absence of power, but upon lodging it with those whom the people can change or continue at stated intervals through an honest and free system of elections.'[135]

A tide of popular favour carried Roosevelt beyond the bounds of constitutional convention when he sought, and won, a third term of office to prosecute the war against the European axis. The revered George Washington had retired after a second term of office and since then it had been taken as an unwritten rule that no president would serve more than two consecutive terms. After Roosevelt's death in office the constitution was amended to turn the two-term restriction into law.

In his third term Roosevelt prepared a new bill of rights that was focused on providing welfare and alleviating poverty. It was clearly of democratic intent. Roosevelt proposed rights to a living wage, to a 'decent home', to medical care, to security in old age or other infirmity, to education.[136] While many seek to besmirch Roosevelt's record, some are prepared to call him 'visionary'.[137] The subtitle of Cass R. Sunstein's book on the subject – why we need Roosevelt's 'revolution' now more than ever – is a renewed cry for control of rampant corporate power. In the early decades of the twentieth century James Bryce discerned 'a new form of tyranny' in which capital interests neutered and took over the role of government in many areas of life.[138]

The situation is probably more dire today than ever before. Recent authors have despaired over the deadlock in the system, as powerful vested interests infiltrate the processes of government and stall the normal flow of policy making. Barack Obama was elected to the presidency in 2008 with high hopes for a benign change in the direction of government. Yet his term has seen the worst of the deadlock in congress, while enormously powerful outside interests line up to thwart his ambitions. We need merely mention his desire to restrict the purchase of guns, only to be shot down by the gun lobby. His introduction of a limited communal health care program has been opposed by the boundlessly powerful pharmaceutical industry, which has managed to persuade many who would benefit most from a comprehensive health scheme to denounce his program as a socialist plot.

Others have called the more or less permanent situation 'gridlock'. Before he had settled into office Obama announced at his first inaugural that politics was 'strangled' by 'petty grievances' and 'worn-out dogmas'. Amy Gutmann and Dennis Thompson assign the problem to the growth of an 'uncompromising mindset', and deplore the campaigning attitude as a 'permanent opposition'.[139] It is true that uncompromising attitudes on opposing sides are in part to blame for the inertia. Yet we should be clear that it has long been understood that the system itself, rooted in the republican tradition, was built for inertia, since no power was allowed to exert too much influence, including the power of the multitude. Long ago James MacGregor Burns analysed the Madison compromise with great care, and declared that the constitution was bound for deadlock. Robert A. Dahl concluded that the constitution itself was pitted against democracy. C.H. McIlwain, although admiring the talent of the founders, noted that while the constitution prevented much evil, it also precluded much good.[140]

One of the most powerful and original thinkers of recent times, Sheldon Wolin, who taught generations of students to appreciate the glories of the world's great political philosophers,[141] finally expressed his exasperation with what the political system of the United States had become. He saw a nation throttled by the stranglehold of the military-industrial-political complex that had fashioned a totalitarian dictatorship over the people. Wolin proposed as an accurate characterization 'inverted totalitarianism'.[142] Totalitarianism applies especially to the total dictatorships in Germany, Italy and Russia around the time of the Second World War. Its characteristic was the complete concentration of power in the state, and the further concentration of the power of the state in a particular leader. All other institutions, churches, guilds, unions, corporations, clubs and associations of all kinds were immediately subject to the power of the state. The leader could annihilate or 'liquidate' any person on any cause or none; or, as Stalin said, if he shook his little finger.

By contrast, inverted totalitarianism uses the power of the state at will, but the sources of power are located well outside the state institutions. With supreme irony, while using the coercive instruments of the state, the private interests controlling it set up a relentless train of propaganda denigrating the state. That is to

71

invalidate the state for any social or democratic purpose and to dissipate popular illusions that the state may exist to help them. Wolin says that this state of affairs is abetted by the ferment of change, technological and institutional (as in education where 'change' is urged on all participants, particularly in the direction of privatizing the means of education). The other side of change is the undermining of consolidation, the dissolution of institutions and the dispersal of the collective wisdom of a people. Inverted totalitarianism thrives on forgetting.

Wolin's frustration was set off particularly by the suspect election of George W. Bush, by the reaction to the devastating attacks on New York and Washington in 2001, and the foolish and destructive invasion of Iraq in revenge for the 9/11 attacks, even though Iraq had nothing to do with them. Wolin's view of the election incorporates the Florida coup, although 'The Florida recount was as much an example of a corporate takeover as of a coup d'état.'[143] The state, propelled by the military-industrial complex, deployed every lie its functionaries could dream up to justify George W. Bush's war. The administration is saturated in 'corporate culture', and shares the aggressive culture of corporate capitalism, which relies on 'creative destruction' as Schumpeter called it. It propagates deceitful euphemisms like 'collateral damage', which essentially means the killing of civilians, especially including women and children, and corporate 'downsizing', which issues in 'careers destroyed, lives radically changed, hopes blasted'.[144]

Tom Keneally, as we saw, recoiled from the realities of American inequality and of poor people living in squalor and without hope. Yet he claimed that this was nothing to do with its being a republic. His view is fundamentally wrong. The 'republic' was a conscious choice of the American framers, and it was fashioned explicitly as a defence against democracy and the forces of equality. The founders divided the world into people of wisdom 'the few' (that is, as Aristotle knew, the rich, the elite) and the people of 'passion', the many. The irrational 'passion' of the many had to be contained by the rationality and wisdom of the few. Yet their 'wisdom' was vested in the vastness of their estates, the aggressiveness of their entrepreneurship, the power of their business, while the retention of their privilege depended on the maintenance of inequality. It might be tempting to characterize Wolin's case as bounded by the more recent rise and super aggression of corporate capitalism, but he is perfectly aware of the historical processes that opened the path to massive accumulation and concentration of wealth and privilege; this was down to the republican constitution.

At the time of the War of Independence against Britain, there were indeed potent democratic forces stirring, as we saw with Wood and Bailyn. Democracy in context 'stood for a politics of redress, for common action to alleviate the sharp inequalities of wealth and power that enabled the more affluent and educated to monopolize governance'. It was this that the founders underplayed as 'folly' and 'turbulence'. But turbulence was the 'demotic form of political dynamics'. It was the action of artisans, labourers, small farmers, small merchants, and foot soldiers. Continued expressions of democracy, as with Jefferson, Jackson, Roosevelt, went 'against the grain, *against the very forms by which the political and economic power of the country has been and continues to be ordered*'.[145]

73

Conclusion

To reconfirm, the central qualification of the historical republic was the removal of the monarchy. The 'people's affair' essentially meant government without a king, but in our two paradigm examples, not actually rule by the people. They demonstrate a concerted effort to maintain the status quo of privilege for the few and an encouraged forgetting for the many, action to thwart democratic movements, a claim to 'virtue' and wisdom on the part of the few, the consolidation of power in private hands, the removal of obstacles to the extension of private power and wealth, and the capture of the reins of state by those who had no respect for constitutional niceties or restraints. In each case the republic began in an uprising in which overbearing monarchy was removed by force.

The Australian republican movement is certainly focused on the removal of the crown and the patriotic installation of an Australian as head of state. There is also much concern about cutting residual imperial ties with Britain, but there has never been any suggestion of a violent uprising against Britain, at least not since Lang in the 1850s. As I have affirmed, there is no moral justification for the permanent rule of a person distinguished merely by heredity, and indeed speculation in Britain may come to a similar conclusion once the present Queen, just turned ninety, expires.

Yet can Australians really claim that they share a revolutionary passion against *oppression* by the monarchy? We indeed have a right to be deeply indignant at any implication of the monarchy in the home-grown dismissal of an elected Australian government, but the real villains there were the local few who claimed the privilege of themselves being born to rule.

Sheldon Wolin's warnings about the reactionary trajectory of the American republic are dire indeed. We can also see the effects of administrations suffused in corporate culture in both Cameron's Britain and Turnbull's Australia. Both prime ministers continue to downgrade the social functions of government, and accelerate the privatization of government institutions and services, a process the American political scientist, Benjamin Barber, called the death of democracy. Turnbull headlines an electoral campaign with the slogan 'jobs and growth', while the coalition government continues drastically to reduce the funds of public institutions, such as education and health care provisions, slashing the jobs of many dedicated public servants. Obviously 'private' jobs are more valued than 'public' ones.

It may fairly be replied that neither Cameron nor Turnbull operates in a republic, and that corporatized politics has become a feature of systems that were designed as parliamentary democracies. Malcolm Turnbull was once an acclaimed republican, but it no longer seems to suit his purposes to acknowledge his past commitments.

One might argue that corporatized democracies that are not republics might not have anything further to fear from republicanism. Yet a brief historical survey of the alpha and omega of republicanism demonstrates that the nature of republicanism is to gravitate against the interests of the public, and to provide obstacles to the people's taking charge of their own affairs.

Again, it may be said, it does not *have* to be like that. Ireland, for example, seems to be a stable, 'democratic' republic. Perhaps not all countries can produce a Mary Robinson, but in any case, the constitution of Ireland that preceded its republican style adopted the form of a constitutional monarchy, replacing the crown with a rotating presidency. Ireland became a republic in 1948 when all reference to the British monarch was removed. Australia would be faced with *creating* a presidency, and working out how to contain it within democratic controls. Undoubtedly we would look to America, as in so much else, and there we would find an example quite alien to our own traditions.

For reasons stated above, Australia cannot now be in a similar position to Ireland's. The advocates who, like Turnbull at his republican prime, said that the republic had nothing to do with anything other than installing an Australian as head of state, were disingenuously embedding a collective amnesia about the course of the greatest republics – an inconvenient truth.

Australia has travelled quite a distance down the path towards a corporatist culture, and already languishes under the incubus of corporate power on progressive movements. The deputy prime-minister, Barnaby Joyce, tells people at the (phoney) beginning of the 2016 election campaign to vote for Malcolm Turnbull as prime minister because he is a successful businessman. But he stands at the heart of oligarchic republicanism, whether he still acknowledges the term or not. It could be hugely detrimental to adopt a political style that carries with it the baggage of relentless entrenchment of the power of the few over the many. We have always looked to America for example, and we are already saturated in American popular culture. Some Australian framers of the constitution, such as Andrew Inglis Clark, would have been happy for Australia to adopt the American constitution holus bolus. Local aspirants to capitalist control of the country might well be happy to take over someone else's history to bolster their ambition. We do not need to borrow an alien political culture that has been built around the aggrandizement of the rich and the immiseration of the poor. Just look at the *working poor* of America, in their millions.

If we must change, let us retain the salutary style of 'Commonwealth',[146] a notion that fully embraces the wellbeing of all the people, but let the advocates of change at least work out how to involve the people without establishing a separate presidency vested with powers to challenge the legislature and threaten deadlock.

Notes

1   Cf. John Warhurst, 'Nationalism and Republicanism in
    Australia: The Evolution of Institutions, Citizenship and
    Symbols', in Stephanie Lawson and Graham Maddox, eds,
    Australia's Republican Question, special edition of *Australian
    Journal of Political Science*, vol. 28, 1993, pp. 100–20.

2   Tom Keneally, *Our Republic*, Port Melbourne, Heinemann,
    1993.

3   George Winterton, 'The Constitutional Implications of a
    Republic' in M.A. Stephenson and Clive Turner, eds, *Australia.
    Republic or Monarchy?*, St Lucia, University of Queensland
    Press, 1994, p. 15–33, at p. 15.

4   Alastair Davidson, '*Res publica* and citizen', in David Headon,
    James Warden & Bill Gammage, eds, *Crown and Country. The
    traditions of Australian republicanism*, St Leonards, Allen &
    Unwin, 1994, pp. 161–74, at p. 161.

5   Eric Nelson, *The Greek Tradition in Republican Thought*,
    Cambridge, Cambridge. University Press, 2004, pp. 4–5.

6   J.B. Paul, quoted in Keneally, *Our Republic*, p. 59; Michael
    Kirby, 'Reflections on Constitutional Monarchy' in Wayne
    Hudson and David Carter eds, *The Republicanism Debate*,
    Kensington, New South Wales University Press, 1993, pp. 61–
    76, at pp. 73–4; David Flint, 'Our crowned republic's crowning
    common sense', *Australians for a Constitutional* Monarchy,
    22 October 2009 http://www.norepublic.com.au/index.
    php?option=com_content&task=view&id=2108&Itemid=6;
    Viewed April 2016. Walter Bagehot, *The English Constitution,*
    M. Taylor, ed., Oxford, Oxford University Press, 2001, p. 48.

7   Helen Irving, 'Who were the Republicans?' in Headon et al., *Crown and Country*, pp. 69–79, at p. 72.

8   I thank Dr Tim Battin for this comment.

9   Malcolm Turnbull, in Hudson and Carter, eds, *Republicanism Debate*, p. 222.

10   Keneally, *Our Republic*, p. 117.

11   Malcolm Turnbull, *The Reluctant Republic*, Port Melbourne, Mandarin, 1994, p. 7.

12   Ibid., p. 11.

13   James Boyd White, *When Words Lose Their Meaning. Constitutions and Reconstitutions of Language, Character and Community*, Chicago, University of Chicago Press, 1984; cf. Terence Ball, James Farr and Russell Hanson (eds), *Political Innovation and Conceptual Change*, Cambridge, Cambridge University Press, 1989.

14   Warhurst, 'Political Studies and the Monarchy', *Politics*, vol. 23, no. 1, 1988, pp. 1–7, at p. 3.

15   Keneally, *Our Republic*, pp. 1–3.

16   Donald Horne et al., *The Coming Republic*, Chippendale, Pan Macmillan, 1992, pp. 20–4.

17   Son of Henry Purcell.

18   1953 Visit of Queen Elizabeth II, *Menzies Virtual Museum*, http://menziesvirtualmuseum.org.au/broadcasts/389-1963-visit-of-queen-elizabeth-ii Viewed 7 April 2016.

19   Myfanwy Gollan talking to Veronica Brady in Horne et al., *Coming Republic*, p. 85.

20   Keneally, *Our Republic*, p. 24.

21   Ibid., p. 35.

22   Brent Waters in Horne et al., *Coming Republic*, p. 172, and citing Geraldine Doogue in the *Telgraph-Mirror*, 19 July 1991.

23   Keneally, *Our Republic*, p. 80, and citing Les Murray, 'The Flag Rave. A personal iconography of the Australian republic', in Geoffrey Dutton, ed., *Republican Australia?*, Melbourne, Sun

Books, 1977, pp. 106–19, at p. 113, emphasis added.

24 Keneally, *Our Republic*, p. 112.

25 Cf. Patrick White, 'A Democratic Australian Republic', in Dutton, ed., *Republican Australia?*, pp. 197–201, at p. 200.

26 Elaine Thompson, 'Giving Ourselves Better Government', in Horne et al., *Coming Republic*, pp. 148–60, at p. 148.

27 Horne, *Coming Republic*, pp. 144–7.

28 Turnbull, *Reluctant Republic*, p. 9

29 Martin Krygier, 'Subjects, objects and the colonial rule of law', in his *Civil Passions*, Melbourne, Black Inc., 2004, pp. 56–91.

30 Patricia Springborg, 'An Historical Note on Republicanism', in Hudson and Carter, eds, *Republicanism Debate,* pp. 201–7, at p. 203.

31 Mark McKenna, *The Captive Republic. A History of republicanism in Australia 1788-1996*, Cambridge, Cambridge University Press, 1996.

32 Ibid., p. 49.

33 Don Baker, 'Good Government and self-government: The republicanism of John Dunmore Lang', in Headon et al. eds, *Crown or Country*, pp. 39-45, at p. 40.

34 Patrick O'Farrell, *The Catholic Church and Community in Australia*, West Melbourne, Nelson, 1977, p. 51.

35 Ibid., p. 38.

36 Baker, *Australian Dictionary of Biography*, vol. 2, s.v. Lang, John Dunmore (1799–1878).

37 McKenna, *Captive Republic,* p. 49.

38 J.D. Lang, *The Coming Event, or Freedom and Independence for the United Provinces of Australia* [1850], Sydney, Sheriff, 1970.

39 McKenna, *Captive Republic*, p. 54.

40 Lang, *Freedom and Independence for the Golden Lands of Australia: the rights of the colonies and the interests of Britain and of the world*, London, Longman, Brown, Green and Longmans, 1852.

41 See e.g. Helen Irving, *To Constitute a Nation*, Cambridge, Cambridge University Press, 1997, p. 49.

42 Graham Maddox and Tod Moore, 'Mainline Calvinists, Pamphlets and Democracy in Revolutionary Britain 1641–1646', in Jim Jose and Robert Imre, eds, *Not So Strange Bedfellows: The Nexus of Politics and Religion in the 21st Century*, Newcastle upon Tyne, Cambridge Scholars Publishing, 2013, pp. 26–44.

43 Gordon S. Wood, *The Radicalism of the American Revolution*, New York, Knopf, 1992, pp. 144–5.

44 Kevin Phillips, *The Cousins' Wars: Religion, Politics and the Triumph of Anglo-America*, New York, Basic Books, 1999, pp. 92, 177, as cited by Richard Gardiner, 'A Presbyterian Rebellion?' *Journal of the American Revolution*, 5 September, 2013.

45 Peter Force, ed., 'Extract of a Letter to a Gentleman in London, from New York, May 31, 1774', *American Archives*, Fourth Series, vol. 1, p. 301, cited Gardiner.

46 Sheldon Wolin, *Democracy Incorporated*, Princeton, Princeton University Press, 2008, p. 130.

47 Wolin, *Democracy Incorporated*, p. 154.

48 Dutton, 'Preface' in Dutton, ed., *Republican Australia*, p. vi.

49 Thompson, 'Better Government'.

50 Cf. John Hirst, *A Republican Manifesto*, Melbourne, Oxford University Press, 1994, pp. 64–71.

51 Turnbull, *Reluctant Republic*, p. 69.

52 Ibid., pp. 106–9.

53 Donald Horne, *Death of The Lucky Country*, Harmondsworth, Penguin, 1976, pp. 44–54.

54 Keneally, *Our Republic*, p. 140.

55 Jeffrey Archer and Graham Maddox, 'The 1975 Constitutional Crisis in Australia', *Journal of Commonwealth and Comparative Politics*, 15, July, 1976, pp. 141–57.

56 Keneally, *Our Republic*, p. 139.

57 Cf. Alan Atkinson, *The Muddle-headed Republic*, Melbourne, Oxford University Press, 1994.

58 Jenny Hocking, *The Dismissal Dossier*, Carlton, Melbourne University Press, 2015, *passim*, and on 'reserve powers', p. 13.

59 Ibid., p. 37.

60 Ibid., pp. 12–26.

61 Winterton, 'The Constitutional Implications of a Republic', in Stephenson and Turner, eds, *Republic or Monarchy?*, p. 15.

62 Winterton, *Monarchy to Republic. Australian Republican Government*, Melbourne, Oxford University Press, 1986.

63 Colin Howard, *Australia's Constitution*, Harmondsworth, Penguin, 1978, p. 45.

64 Gregory Melleuish, 'Republicanism Before Nationalism', in Hudson and Carter, eds, *Republicanism Debate*, pp. 77–87.

65 Wayne Hudson, 'Republicanism and Utopianism', pp. 158–76; Alastair Davidson, Republicanism and Democratic Reform', pp. 97–108; cf. Andrew Fraser, 'Strong Republicanism and a Citizens' Constitution'; pp. 36–60, all in Hudson and Carter, eds, *Republicanism Debate*.

66 Patricia Springborg, *Western Republicanism and the Oriental Prince*, Cambridge, Polity, 1992, p. 185.

67 Bill Brugger, *Republican Theory in Political Thought. Virtuous or Virtual?*, Basingstoke, Macmillan, 1999, p. 181.

68 Philip Pettit, *Republicanism. A Theory of Freedom and Government*, Oxford, Clarendon Press, 1997.

69 Keneally, *Our Republic*, p. 209, emphasis added.

70 Springborg, *Western Republicanism*, p. 280.

71 Mary Beard, *SPQR. A history of ancient Rome*, London, Profile Books, 2016, pp. 117–28.

72 Livy, *Ab Urbe Condita* (From the Founding of the City), 2. 44. 9.

73 Beard, *SPQR*, p. 167.

74 Hanna Pitkin, 'Are freedom and Liberty "Twins"?', *Political Theory*, pp. 523–52, at pp. 534–5.

75 Polybius, *Histories*, 2. 21.

76 F.B. Marsh, 'In Defense of the Corn-Dole', *Classical Journal*, vol. 22, no. 1, 1926, pp. 10–25, at p. 24.

77 P.A. Brunt, *Social Conflicts in the Roman Republic*, London, Chatto & Windus, 1971, p. 89.

78 Michal Crawford, *The Roman Republic*, Glasgow, Fontana, 1978, pp. 115–23.

79 Brunt, *Social Conflicts*, pp. 6–9.

80 Ibid., p. 92.

81 Von Scala, quoted by F.W. Walbank, 'Polybius on the Roman Constitution', *Classical Quarterly*, vol. 37, nos 3/4, 1943, pp. 73–89, at p. 89.

82 Brunt, 'The Army and the Land in the Roman Revolution', *Journal of Roman Studies*, vol. 52, nos 1 & 2, 1962, pp. 69-86, at p. 71.

83 Brunt, *Social Conflicts*, p. 97.

84 Crawford, *Roman Republic*, p. 127.

85 A.N. Sherwin-White, 'Violence in Roman Politics', *Journal of Roman Studies*, vol. 46, nos 1 & 2, 1956, pp. 1–9, at p. 5.

86 Brunt, *Social Conflicts*, p. 107.

87 H.H. Scullard, *From the Gracchi to Nero*, London, Methuen, 1963, p. 81.

88 Lily Ross Taylor, *Party Politics in the Age of Caesar,* Berkeley and Los Angeles, University of California Press, 1971, p. 15.

89 Suetonius, *Divus Julius*, 77.

90 Brunt, *Social Conflicts*, p. 143.

91 Mary T. Boatwright, Daniel L. Gargola, Noel Lenski and Richard J.A. Talbert, *The Romans from Village to Empire*, New York, Oxford University Press, 2012, pp. 276–7.

92 Cicero, *De Legibus* 1. 56.

93 Graham Maddox, 'The Secular Reformation and the Influence of Machiavelli', *Journal of Religion* (Chicago), 82, 4, Oct. 2002, pp. 539–62.

94 F.W. Walbank, *Polybius*, Berkeley and Los Angeles, University of California Press, 1972, p. 156.

95 Cicero, *Pro Setio*, 99.

96 Brunt, *Social Conflicts*, p. 138, emphasis added.

97 J.P.V.D. Balsdon 'Auctoritas, Dignitas, Otium', *Classical Quarterly*, vol. 10, no. 1, 1960, pp. 43–50, at p. 47.

98 Cicero, *De Legibus*, 3. 19.

99 Bernard Bailyn, *The Ideological Origins of the American Revolution*, Cambridge, Mass.: Belknap Press, 1967, p. 230.

100 John Winthrop, 'Modell of Christian Charity', [1630] in Perry Miller and Thomas H. Johnson (eds), *The Puritans*, two vols, New York, rev. ed., 1963, p. 198.

101 John Cotton, *The Way of Congregational Churches Cleared*, London, 1648, p. 97.

102 Gordon S. Wood, *The American Revolution: A History*, New York: Random House, 2003, p. 152.

103 J.G.A. Pocock, *The Machiavellian Moment*, Princeton: Princeton University Press, 1975, pp. 31–48; for Jefferson's use of 'a revolution of the wheel of fortune', see e.g. Willard S. Randall, *Thomas Jefferson: A Life*, New York: HarperCollins, 1994, p. 301.

104 Cf. Thomas L. Pangle, *The Spirit of Modern Republicanism. The Moral Vision of the American Founders and the Philosophy of Locke*, Chicago, University of Chicago Press, 1988, p. 8.

105 Ibid., pp. 30–1.

106 Charles A. Beard, *An Economic Interpretation of the Constitution of the United States*, New York: Free Press, new ed., 1986, p. 154.

107 James Madison, *The Federalist No. 10*, in Clinton Rossiter ed. *The Federalist Papers*, New York, Mentor, 1961, pp. 81–4.

108 John Adams, 'A defence of the constitutions of government of

the United States of America' [1786–87], in George A. Peek, Jr (ed.), *The Political Writings of John Adams: Representative Selections*, Indianapolis, Liberal Arts Press, 1964, p. 149.

109 Alexander Hamilton, *Federalist No. 6*, in Rossiter, ed., p. 54.

110 Cf. John Uhr, 'Instituting Republicanism: Parliamentary Vices, Republican Virtues?', in Lawson and Maddox eds, *Republican Question,* pp. 27–39, at. pp. 29–31.

111 Madison, *Federalist No. 49,* in Rossiter, ed., p. 315.

112 G. Maddox, 'The Influence of Machiavelli'.

113 Pangle, *Spirit of Republicanism*, p. 30.

114 Daniel J. Boorstin, *The Democratic Experience*, New York: Random House, 1973, p. 390.

115 Joyce Appleby, 'Republicanism in old and new contexts', *William and Mary Quarterly*, vol. 43, 1986, pp. 20–34, at p. 25.

116 Joseph A. Schumpeter, *Capitalism, Socialism and Democracy*, London, Unwin, 5th ed., 1952, p. 269.

117 See e.g. Bernard Berelson et al., *Voting*, Chicago: University of Chicago Press, 1954.

118 Lance Banning, *The Jeffersonian Persuasion*, Ithaca: Cornell University Press, 1978, p. 273.

119 Quoted in James MacGregor Burns, *The Deadlock of Democracy*, Englewood Cliffs, Prentice Hall, 1963, p. 38.

120 Banning, *Jeffersonian Persuasion*, p. 148.

121 Wood, *The Radicalism of the American Revolution*, New York: Knopf, 1992, p. 331.

122 Sean Wilentz, *The Rise of American Democracy*, New York: Norton, 2005, p. 272.

123 Russell Hanson, 'Democracy', in Ball, Farr and Hanson (eds), *Political Innovation and Conceptual Change*, pp. 68–89, at p. 78.

124 Andrew Jackson, quoted ibid., p. 370.

125 Arthur M. Schlesinger Jr, *The Age of Jackson*, Boston: Little, Brown, 1945, p. 308.

126 Robert A. Dahl, *How Democratic is the American Constitution?*, New Haven, Yale University Press, 2nd ed., 2003, p. 69.

127 Richard Hofstadter, *The American Political Tradition*, London, Jonathan Cape, 1967, p. 49.

128 Wilentz, *Rise of American Democracy*, p. 312.

129 Cornel West, *Democracy Matters*, New York, Penguin, 2004, p. 49.

130 Reinhold Niebuhr, *The Children of Light and the Children of Darkness*, New York, Scribner's, 1944, p. 95.

131 Ronald Reagan, *An American Life*, New York, Simon & Schuster, 1990, p. 67.

132 Nicholas Wapshott, *The Clash that Defined Economics: Keynes. Hayek*, Melbourne: Scribe, 2011, pp. 158–9.

133 S.E. Morison and H.S. Commager, *The Growth of the American Republic*, New York, Oxford University Press, 1962, two vols, vol. 2, p. 732.

134 Franklin D. Roosevelt, 'Greeting to the Economic Club of New York', December 1940, as quoted in Morton J. Frisch, 'Franklin D. Roosevelt and the problem of democratic liberty', *Ethics*, vol. 73, no. 3, 1962, pp. 180–92, at p. 185.

135 Ibid., p. 183.

136 Cass R. Sunstein, *The Second Bill of Rights: FDR's Unfinished Revolution and Why We Need It More than Ever*, New York, Basic Books, 2004, pp, 242–3.

137 James T. Kloppenberg, 'Franklin Delano Roosevelt, visionary', *Reviews in American History*, vol. 34, 2006, pp. 509–20, at p. 519.

138 James Bryce, *The American Commonwealth*, New York, Putnam's Sons, 1959, two vols, vol. 2, pp. 400–1.

139 Amy Gutmann and Dennis Thompson, *The Spirit of Compromise: Why Government Demands It and Campaigning Undermines It*, Princeton, Princeton University Press, 2012.

140 James MacGregor Burns, *The Deadlock of Democracy*, Englewood Cliffs, Prentice-Hall, 1963; Robert A. Dahl, *How*

Democratic is the American Constitution?, New Haven:, Yale University Press, 2002; C.H. McIlwain, *Constitutionalism in the Changing World*, Cambridge, Cambridge University Press, 1939.

141 Sheldon S. Wolin, *Politics and Vision. Continuity and innovation in Western political thought*, Boston, Little, Brown, 1960.

142 Wolin, *Democracy Incorporated. Managed democracy and the specter of inverted totalitarianism*, Princeton, Princeton University Press, 2008.

143 Ibid., p. 102.

144 Ibid., pp. 143–4.

145 Ibid., pp. 227–8, emphasis added.

146 David Wells, *In defence of the common wealth. Reflections on Australian politics,* Melbourne, Longman Cheshire, 1990.